Mother's Day
5/11/14
from Mark

God's
Promises®
for Women

NIV

by Jack Countryman

[COUNTRYMAN]®

A Division of Thomas Nelson Publishers

THOMAS NELSON
Since 1798

NASHVILLE DALLAS MEXICO CITY RIO DE JANEIRO

Contents

Introduction

Women are one of the jewels of God's creation—an expression of His love. Throughout the Old and New Testament, God's promises speak specifically to the love, mercy, and grace our heavenly Father gives women. This book has been created to give you direction, comfort, and encouragement to meet the challenges you face in life. May *God's Promises® for Women NIV* be a blessing to you in your daily walk.

God's Plan
for Women
Is *to* . . .

Worship Him

Ascribe to the LORD, you heavenly beings,
    ascribe to the LORD glory and strength.
Ascribe to the LORD the glory due his name;
    worship the LORD in the splendor of his holiness.

PSALM 29:1–2

Come, let us bow down in worship,
    let us kneel before the LORD our Maker;
for he is our God
    and we are the people of his pasture,
    the flock under his care.

PSALM 95:6–7

"Yet a time is coming and has now come when the true worshipers will worship the Father in the Spirit and in truth, for they are the kind of worshipers the Father seeks. God is spirit, and his worshipers must worship in the Spirit and in truth."

JOHN 4:23–24

Ascribe to the LORD, all you families of nations,
    ascribe to the LORD glory and strength.
Ascribe to the LORD the glory due his name;
    bring an offering and come into his courts.
Worship the LORD in the splendor of his holiness;
    tremble before him, all the earth.
Say among the nations, "The LORD reigns."
    The world is firmly established, it cannot be
        moved;
    he will judge the peoples with equity.

PSALM 96:7–10

Look to the LORD and his strength;
    seek his face always.
Remember the wonders he has done,
    his miracles, and the judgments he pronounced,
you his servants, the descendants of Israel,
    his chosen ones, the children of Jacob.
He is the LORD our God;
    his judgments are in all the earth.

1 CHRONICLES 16:11–14

Blessed are those who keep his statutes
and seek him with all their heart. . . .
I seek you with all my heart;
do not let me stray from your commands.
I have hidden your word in my heart
that I might not sin against you.

PSALM 119:2, 10–11

I will praise you as long as I live,
and in your name I will lift up my hands.
I will be fully satisfied as with the richest of foods;
with singing lips my mouth will praise you. . . .
Because you are my help,
I sing in the shadow of your wings.
I cling to you;
your right hand upholds me.

PSALM 63:4–5, 7–8

Obey Him

Do not merely listen to the word, and so deceive yourselves. Do what it says. Anyone who listens to the word but does not do what it says is like someone who looks at his face in a mirror and, after looking at himself, goes away and immediately forgets what he looks like. But whoever looks intently into the perfect law that gives freedom, and continues in it—not forgetting what they have heard, but doing it—they will be blessed in what they do.

JAMES 1:22–25

"Whoever can be trusted with very little can also be trusted with much, and whoever is dishonest with very little will also be dishonest with much. . . . No one can serve two masters. Either you will hate the one and love the other, or you will be devoted to the one and despise the other. You cannot serve both God and money."

LUKE 16:10, 13

"Why do you call me, 'Lord, Lord,' and do not do what I say? As for everyone who comes to me and hears my words and puts them into practice, I will show you what they are like. They are like a man building a house, who dug down deep and laid the foundation on rock. When a flood came, the torrent struck that house but could not shake it, because it was well built. But the one who hears my words and does not put them into practice is like a man who built a house on the ground without a foundation. The moment the torrent struck that house, it collapsed and its destruction was complete."

LUKE 6:46–49

Moreover, we have all had human fathers who disciplined us and we respected them for it. How much more should we submit to the Father of spirits and live! They disciplined us for a little while as they thought best; but God disciplines us for our good, in order that we may share in his holiness. No discipline seems pleasant at the time, but painful. Later on, however, it produces a harvest of righteousness and peace for those who have been trained by it.

HEBREWS 12:9–11

"If you love me, keep my commands. And I will ask the Father, and he will give you another advocate to help you and be with you forever."

John 14:15–16

Do not love the world or anything in the world. If anyone loves the world, love for the Father is not in them. For everything in the world—the lust of the flesh, the lust of the eyes, and the pride of life—comes not from the Father but from the world. The world and its desires pass away, but whoever does the will of God lives forever.

1 John 2:15–17

You need to persevere so that when you have done the will of God, you will receive what he has promised. For,

> "In just a little while,
>> he who is coming will come
>> and will not delay."

And,

> "But my righteous one will live by faith.
>> And I take no pleasure
>> in the one who shrinks back."

Hebrews 10:36–38

Come to Him in Prayer

Therefore, since we have a great high priest who has ascended into heaven, Jesus the Son of God, let us hold firmly to the faith we profess. For we do not have a high priest who is unable to empathize with our weaknesses, but we have one who has been tempted in every way, just as we are—yet he did not sin. Let us then approach God's throne of grace with confidence, so that we may receive mercy and find grace to help us in our time of need.

HEBREWS 4:14–16

For the eyes of the Lord are on the righteous
        and his ears are attentive to their prayer,
            but the face of the Lord is against those who
                do evil.

1 PETER 3:12

As for me, I call to God,
    and the LORD saves me.
Evening, morning and noon
    I cry out in distress,
    and he hears my voice. . . .
Cast your cares on the LORD
    and he will sustain you;
    he will never let
    the righteous be shaken.

PSALM 55:16–17, 22

Hear my prayer, LORD;
    listen to my cry for mercy.
When I am in distress, I call to you,
    because you answer me. . . .
For you are great and do marvelous deeds;
    you alone are God.

PSALM 86:6–7, 10

"Call to me and I will answer you and tell you great and unsearchable things you do not know."

JEREMIAH 33:3

9

Do not be anxious about anything, but in every situation, by prayer and petition, with thanksgiving, present your requests to God. And the peace of God, which transcends all understanding, will guard your hearts and your minds in Christ Jesus.

PHILIPPIANS 4:6–7

"And when you pray, do not be like the hypocrites, for they love to pray standing in the synagogues and on the street corners to be seen by others. Truly I tell you, they have received their reward in full. But when you pray, go into your room, close the door and pray to your Father, who is unseen. Then your Father, who sees what is done in secret, will reward you."

MATTHEW 6:5–6

You will pray to him, and he will hear you,
    and you will fulfill your vows.
What you decide on will be done,
    and light will shine on your ways.

JOB 22:27–28

Listen to the Holy Spirit

The Spirit searches all things, even the deep things of God. For who knows a person's thoughts except their own spirit within them? In the same way no one knows the thoughts of God except the Spirit of God. What we have received is not the spirit of the world, but the Spirit who is from God, so that we may understand what God has freely given us. This is what we speak, not in words taught us by human wisdom but in words taught by the Spirit, explaining spiritual realities with Spirit-taught words.

1 CORINTHIANS 2:10–13

But you, dear friends, by building yourselves up in your most holy faith and praying in the Holy Spirit, keep yourselves in God's love as you wait for the mercy of our Lord Jesus Christ to bring you to eternal life.

JUDE VV. 20–21

And if the Spirit of him who raised Jesus from the dead is living in you, he who raised Christ from the dead will also give life to your mortal bodies because of his Spirit who lives in you. . . .

The Spirit himself testifies with our spirit that we are God's children. Now if we are children, then we are heirs—heirs of God and co-heirs with Christ, if indeed we share in his sufferings in order that we may also share in his glory.

I consider that our present sufferings are not worth comparing with the glory that will be revealed in us. . . .

In the same way, the Spirit helps us in our weakness. We do not know what we ought to pray for, but the Spirit himself intercedes for us through wordless groans. And he who searches our hearts knows the mind of the Spirit, because the Spirit intercedes for God's people in accordance with the will of God.

ROMANS 8:11, 16–18, 26–27

"The world cannot accept [the Spirit of truth], because it neither sees him nor knows him. But you know him, for he lives with you and will be in you. I will not leave you as orphans; I will come to you. Before long, the world will not see me anymore, but you will see me. Because I live, you also will live."

JOHN 14:17–19

In him we were also chosen, having been predestined according to the plan of him who works out everything in conformity with the purpose of his will, in order that we, who were the first to put our hope in Christ, might be for the praise of his glory. And you also were included in Christ when you heard the message of truth, the gospel of your salvation. When you believed, you were marked in him with a seal, the promised Holy Spirit, who is a deposit guaranteeing our inheritance until the redemption of those who are God's possession—to the praise of his glory.

EPHESIANS 1:11–14

But you have an anointing from the Holy One, and all of you know the truth. . . . As for you, the anointing you received from him remains in you, and you do not need anyone to teach you. But as his anointing teaches you about all things and as that anointing is real, not counterfeit—just as it has taught you, remain in him.

1 JOHN 2:20, 27

God Teaches
Women *to* Walk
in His Word
by . . .

Praising His Might

Praise the LORD.

    Sing to the LORD a new song,

      his praise in the assembly of his faithful people. . . .

For the LORD takes delight in his people;

    he crowns the humble with victory.

Let his faithful people rejoice in this honor

    and sing for joy on their beds.

PSALM 149:1, 4–5

Praise the LORD.

    Give thanks to the LORD, for he is good;

      his love endures forever.

Who can proclaim the mighty acts of the LORD

    or fully declare his praise?

Blessed are those who act justly,

    who always do what is right.

PSALM 106:1–3

Praise the LORD.

    Praise the LORD, you his servants;
    praise the name of the LORD.
Let the name of the LORD be praised,
    both now and forevermore.
From the rising of the sun to the place where it sets,
    the name of the LORD is to be praised.

PSALM 113:1–3

I will praise God's name in song
    and glorify him with thanksgiving.
This will please the LORD more than an ox,
    more than a bull with its horns and hooves.
The poor will see and be glad—
    you who seek God, may your hearts live!

PSALM 69:30–32

Great is the LORD, and most worthy of praise,
    in the city of our God, his holy mountain.

PSALM 48:1

My heart, O God, is steadfast,
my heart is steadfast;
I will sing and make music.
Awake, my soul!
Awake, harp and lyre!
I will awaken the dawn.
I will praise you, Lord, among the nations;
I will sing of you among the peoples.
For great is your love, reaching to the heavens;
your faithfulness reaches to the skies.

PSALM 57:7–10

Praise the LORD.
Praise the LORD, my soul.
I will praise the LORD all my life;
I will sing praise to my God as long as I live. . . .
Blessed are those whose help is the God of Jacob,
whose hope is in the LORD their God.

PSALM 146:1–2, 5

GOD TEACHES WOMEN TO WALK IN HIS WORD BY . . .

Trusting in His Power

You will keep in perfect peace
    those whose minds are steadfast,
    because they trust in you.
Trust in the LORD forever,
    for the LORD, the LORD himself, is the Rock
        eternal.

ISAIAH 26:3–4

Surely God is my salvation;
    I will trust and not be afraid.
    The LORD, the LORD himself, is my strength and
        my defense;
    he has become my salvation.
With joy you will draw water
    from the wells of salvation.

ISAIAH 12:2–3

In you, LORD, I have taken refuge;
   let me never be put to shame. . . .
Be my rock of refuge,
   to which I can always go;
   give the command to save me,
   for you are my rock and my fortress. . . .
For you have been my hope, Sovereign LORD,
   my confidence since my youth. . . .
My mouth is filled with your praise,
   declaring your splendor all day long.

PSALM 71:1, 3, 5, 8

Indeed, we felt we had received the sentence of death. But this happened that we might not rely on ourselves but on God, who raises the dead. He has delivered us from such a deadly peril, and he will deliver us again. On him we have set our hope that he will continue to deliver us.

2 CORINTHIANS 1:9–10

But if anyone obeys his word, love for God is truly made complete in them. This is how we know we are in him: Whoever claims to live in him must live as Jesus did.

1 JOHN 2:5–6

Whoever does not love does not know God, because God is love. This is how God showed his love among us: He sent his one and only Son into the world that we might live through him. This is love: not that we loved God, but that he loved us and sent his Son as an atoning sacrifice for our sins.

1 JOHN 4:8–10

For Christ's love compels us, because we are convinced that one died for all, and therefore all died. And he died for all, that those who live should no longer live for themselves but for him who died for them and was raised again.

2 CORINTHIANS 5:14–15

In fact, this is love for God: to keep his commands. And his commands are not burdensome, for everyone born of God overcomes the world. This is the victory that has overcome the world, even our faith. Who is it that overcomes the world? Only the one who believes that Jesus is the Son of God.

1 JOHN 5:3–5

Jesus replied: "'Love the Lord your God with all your heart and with all your soul and with all your mind.' This is the first and greatest commandment. And the second is like it: 'Love your neighbor as yourself.' All the Law and the Prophets hang on these two commandments."

MATTHEW 22:37–40

For the Spirit God gave us does not make us timid, but gives us power, love and self-discipline. . . . He has saved us and called us to a holy life—not because of anything we have done but because of his own purpose and grace. This grace was given us in Christ Jesus before the beginning of time.

2 TIMOTHY 1:7, 9

Praying for His Will

Praise be to you, LORD;
> teach me your decrees.
With my lips I recount
> all the laws that come from your mouth.
I rejoice in following your statutes
> as one rejoices in great riches.
I meditate on your precepts
> and consider your ways.
I delight in your decrees;
> I will not neglect your word.

PSALM 119:12–16

Take the helmet of salvation and the sword of the Spirit, which is the word of God. And pray in the Spirit on all occasions with all kinds of prayers and requests. With this in mind, be alert and always keep on praying for all the Lord's people.

EPHESIANS 6:17–18

"Therefore I tell you, whatever you ask for in prayer, believe that you have received it, and it will be yours. And when you stand praying, if you hold anything against anyone, forgive them, so that your Father in heaven may forgive you your sins."

MARK 11:24–25

The LORD is far from the wicked,
   but he hears the prayer of the righteous.

PROVERBS 15:29

The important thing is that in every way, whether from false motives or true, Christ is preached. And because of this I rejoice. Yes, and I will continue to rejoice, for I know that through your prayers and God's provision of the Spirit of Jesus Christ what has happened to me will turn out for my deliverance.

PHILIPPIANS 1:18–19

By day the LORD directs his love,
     at night his song is with me—
     a prayer to the God of my life.

PSALM 42:8

Now when Daniel learned that the decree had been published, he went home to his upstairs room where the windows opened toward Jerusalem. Three times a day he got down on his knees and prayed, giving thanks to his God, just as he had done before.

DANIEL 6:10

Listen to my words, LORD,
     consider my lament.
Hear my cry for help,
     my King and my God,
     for to you I pray.
In the morning, LORD, you hear my voice;
     in the morning I lay my requests before you
     and wait expectantly. . . .
Surely, LORD, you bless the righteous;
     you surround them with your favor as with a shield.

PSALM 5:1–3, 12

GOD TEACHES WOMEN TO WALK IN HIS WORD BY . . .

Following His Light

Do your best to present yourself to God as one approved, a worker who does not need to be ashamed and who correctly handles the word of truth. Avoid godless chatter, because those who indulge in it will become more and more ungodly.

2 TIMOTHY 2:15–16

I have hidden your word in my heart
    that I might not sin against you.
Praise be to you, LORD;
    teach me your decrees.
With my lips I recount
    all the laws that come from your mouth.
I rejoice in following your statutes
    as one rejoices in great riches.

PSALM 119:11–14

Watch out that you do not lose what we have worked for, but that you may be rewarded fully. Anyone who runs ahead and does not continue in the teaching of Christ does not have God; whoever continues in the teaching has both the Father and the Son.

2 JOHN vv. 8–9

"You are the light of the world. A town built on a hill cannot be hidden. Neither do people light a lamp and put it under a bowl. Instead they put it on its stand, and it gives light to everyone in the house. In the same way, let your light shine before others, that they may see your good deeds and glorify your Father in heaven."

MATTHEW 5:14–16

The LORD is my light and my salvation—
    whom shall I fear?
    The LORD is the stronghold of my life—
    of whom shall I be afraid?

PSALM 27:1

Send me your light and your faithful care,
    let them lead me;
    let them bring me to your holy mountain,
    to the place where you dwell.
Then I will go to the altar of God,
    to God, my joy and my delight.
    I will praise you with the lyre,
    O God, my God.

PSALM 43:3–4

Blessed is he who comes in the name of the LORD.
    From the house of the LORD we bless you.
The LORD is God,
    and he has made his light shine on us.
    With boughs in hand, join in the festal procession
    up to the horns of the altar.

PSALM 118:26–27

The light of the righteous shines brightly,
    but the lamp of the wicked is snuffed out.

PROVERBS 13:9

Rejoicing Day and Night

The law of the LORD is perfect,
 refreshing the soul.
 The statutes of the LORD are trustworthy,
 making wise the simple.
The precepts of the LORD are right,
 giving joy to the heart.
 The commands of the LORD are radiant,
 giving light to the eyes. . . .
They are more precious than gold,
 than much pure gold;
 they are sweeter than honey,
 than honey from the honeycomb.

PSALM 19:7–8, 10

Rejoice in the Lord always. I will say it again: Rejoice!
Let your gentleness be evident to all. The Lord is near.

PHILIPPIANS 4:4–5

Sing joyfully to the LORD, you righteous;
>   it is fitting for the upright to praise him.
Praise the LORD with the harp;
>   make music to him on the ten-stringed lyre.
Sing to him a new song;
>   play skillfully, and shout for joy.
For the word of the LORD is right and true;
>   he is faithful in all he does.

PSALM 33:1–4

Let those who love the LORD hate evil,
>   for he guards the lives of his faithful ones
>   and delivers them from the hand of the wicked.
Light shines on the righteous
>   and joy on the upright in heart.
Rejoice in the LORD, you who are righteous,
>   and praise his holy name.

PSALM 97:10–12

I delight greatly in the LORD;
>   my soul rejoices in my God.
>   For he has clothed me with garments of salvation
>   and arrayed me in a robe of his righteousness,

as a bridegroom adorns his head like a priest,
and as a bride adorns herself with her jewels.

ISAIAH 61:10

Yet I will rejoice in the LORD,
    I will be joyful in God my Savior.
The Sovereign LORD is my strength;
      he makes my feet like the feet of a deer,
      he enables me to tread on the heights.

HABAKKUK 3:18–19

But let all who take refuge in you be glad;
      let them ever sing for joy.
      Spread your protection over them,
      that those who love your name may rejoice in you.

PSALM 5:11

Rejoice with those who rejoice; mourn with those who mourn. Live in harmony with one another. Do not be proud, but be willing to associate with people of low position. Do not be conceited.

ROMANS 12:15–16

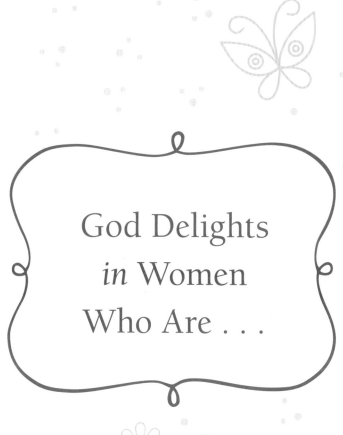

God Delights
in Women
Who Are . . .

Seeking Him

You, God, are my God,
 earnestly I seek you;
 I thirst for you,
 my whole being longs for you,
 in a dry and parched land
 where there is no water.
I have seen you in the sanctuary
 and beheld your power and your glory.
Because your love is better than life,
 my lips will glorify you.
I will praise you as long as I live,
 and in your name I will lift up my hands.

PSALM 63:1–4

I love those who love me,
 and those who seek me find me.

PROVERBS 8:17

Look to the LORD and his strength;
    seek his face always.
Remember the wonders he has done,
    his miracles, and the judgments he pronounced,
you his servants, the descendants of Israel,
    his chosen ones, the children of Jacob.
He is the LORD our God;
    his judgments are in all the earth.

1 CHRONICLES 16:11–14

But if from there you seek the LORD your God, you will find him if you seek him with all your heart and with all your soul. . . . For the LORD your God is a merciful God; he will not abandon or destroy you or forget the covenant with your ancestors, which he confirmed to them by oath.

DEUTERONOMY 4:29, 31

"Ask and it will be given to you; seek and you will find; knock and the door will be opened to you. For everyone who asks receives; the one who seeks finds; and to the one who knocks, the door will be opened."

MATTHEW 7:7–8

I sought the LORD, and he answered me;
    he delivered me from all my fears.
Those who look to him are radiant;
    their faces are never covered with shame.
This poor man called, and the LORD heard him;
    he saved him out of all his troubles.
The angel of the LORD encamps around those who fear
      him,
    and he delivers them.

PSALM 34:4–7

Give praise to the LORD, proclaim his name;
    make known among the nations what he has done.
Sing to him, sing praise to him;
    tell of all his wonderful acts.
Glory in his holy name;
    let the hearts of those who seek the LORD rejoice.
Look to the LORD and his strength;
    seek his face always.

PSALM 105:1–4

Confident in Him

For everything that was written in the past was written to teach us, so that through the endurance taught in the Scriptures and the encouragement they provide we might have hope.

May the God who gives endurance and encouragement give you the same attitude of mind toward each other that Christ Jesus had, so that with one mind and one voice you may glorify the God and Father of our Lord Jesus Christ.

ROMANS 15:4–6

Therefore we are always confident and know that as long as we are at home in the body we are away from the Lord. For we live by faith, not by sight. We are confident, I say, and would prefer to be away from the body and at home with the Lord. So we make it our goal to please him, whether we are at home in the body or away from it.

2 CORINTHIANS 5:6–9

Through Jesus, therefore, let us continually offer to God a sacrifice of praise—the fruit of lips that openly profess his name. And do not forget to do good and to share with others, for with such sacrifices God is pleased.

Have confidence in your leaders and submit to their authority, because they keep watch over you as those who must give an account. Do this so that their work will be a joy, not a burden, for that would be of no benefit to you.

HEBREWS 13:15–17

Though an army besiege me,
 my heart will not fear;
 though war break out against me,
 even then I will be confident.
One thing I ask from the LORD,
 this only do I seek:
 that I may dwell in the house of the LORD
 all the days of my life,
 to gaze on the beauty of the LORD
 and to seek him in his temple.

PSALM 27:3–4

When you lie down, you will not be afraid;
   when you lie down, your sleep will be sweet.
Have no fear of sudden disaster
   or of the ruin that overtakes the wicked,
for the LORD will be at your side
   and will keep your foot from being snared.

PROVERBS 3:24–26

This is the confidence we have in approaching God: that if we ask anything according to his will, he hears us. And if we know that he hears us—whatever we ask—we know that we have what we asked of him.

1 JOHN 5:14–15

We have confidence in the Lord that you are doing and will continue to do the things we command. May the Lord direct your hearts into God's love and Christ's perseverance.

2 THESSALONIANS 3:4–5

GOD DELIGHTS IN WOMEN WHO ARE . . .

Forgiven by Him

Praise the LORD, my soul,
 and forget not all his benefits—
who forgives all your sins
 and heals all your diseases,
who redeems your life from the pit
 and crowns you with love and compassion,
who satisfies your desires with good things
 so that your youth is renewed like the eagle's.

PSALM 103:2–5

For as high as the heavens are above the earth,
 so great is his love for those who fear him;
as far as the east is from the west,
 so far has he removed our transgressions from us.

PSALM 103:11–12

Do not let any unwholesome talk come out of your mouths, but only what is helpful for building others up according to their needs, that it may benefit those who listen. And do not grieve the Holy Spirit of God, with whom you were sealed for the day of redemption. Get rid of all bitterness, rage and anger, brawling and slander, along with every form of malice. Be kind and compassionate to one another, forgiving each other, just as in Christ God forgave you.

EPHESIANS 4:29–32

Bear with each other and forgive one another if any of you has a grievance against someone. Forgive as the Lord forgave you. And over all these virtues put on love, which binds them all together in perfect unity.

COLOSSIANS 3:13–14

When you were dead in your sins and in the uncircumcision of your flesh, God made you alive with Christ. He forgave us all our sins, having canceled the charge of our legal indebtedness, which stood against us and condemned us; he has taken it away, nailing it to the cross.

COLOSSIANS 2:13–14

For he has rescued us from the dominion of darkness and brought us into the kingdom of the Son he loves, in whom we have redemption, the forgiveness of sins.

COLOSSIANS 1:13–14

In him we have redemption through his blood, the forgiveness of sins, in accordance with the riches of God's grace that he lavished on us. With all wisdom and understanding, he made known to us the mystery of his will according to his good pleasure, which he purposed in Christ.

EPHESIANS 1:7–9

If we claim to be without sin, we deceive ourselves and the truth is not in us. If we confess our sins, he is faithful and just and will forgive us our sins and purify us from all unrighteousness.

1 JOHN 1:8–9

GOD DELIGHTS IN WOMEN WHO ARE . . .

Growing in Him

I will instruct you and teach you in the way you
should go;
I will counsel you with my loving eye on you.

PSALM 32:8

So Christ himself gave the apostles, the prophets, the
evangelists, the pastors and teachers, to equip his people for works of service, so that the body of Christ may
be built up until we all reach unity in the faith and in
the knowledge of the Son of God and become mature,
attaining to the whole measure of the fullness of Christ.

Then we will no longer be infants, tossed back and
forth by the waves, and blown here and there by every
wind of teaching and by the cunning and craftiness of
people in their deceitful scheming. Instead, speaking the
truth in love, we will grow to become in every respect
the mature body of him who is the head, that is, Christ.

EPHESIANS 4:11–15

Do not merely listen to the word, and so deceive yourselves. Do what it says. Anyone who listens to the word but does not do what it says is like someone who looks at his face in a mirror and, after looking at himself, goes away and immediately forgets what he looks like. But whoever looks intently into the perfect law that gives freedom, and continues in it—not forgetting what they have heard, but doing it—they will be blessed in what they do.

JAMES 1:22–25

"I am the vine; you are the branches. If you remain in me and I in you, you will bear much fruit; apart from me you can do nothing. If you do not remain in me, you are like a branch that is thrown away and withers; such branches are picked up, thrown into the fire and burned. If you remain in me and my words remain in you, ask whatever you wish, and it will be done for you. This is to my Father's glory, that you bear much fruit, showing yourselves to be my disciples."

JOHN 15:5–8

"Keep this Book of the Law always on your lips; meditate on it day and night, so that you may be careful to do everything written in it. Then you will be prosperous and successful. Have I not commanded you? Be strong and courageous. Do not be afraid; do not be discouraged, for the LORD your God will be with you wherever you go."

JOSHUA 1:8–9

Therefore, dear friends, since you have been forewarned, be on your guard so that you may not be carried away by the error of the lawless and fall from your secure position. But grow in the grace and knowledge of our Lord and Savior Jesus Christ. To him be glory both now and forever! Amen.

2 PETER 3:17–18

"You did not choose me, but I chose you and appointed you so that you might go and bear fruit—fruit that will last—and so that whatever you ask in my name the Father will give you."

JOHN 15:16

Serving Him

"Anyone who loves their life will lose it, while anyone who hates their life in this world will keep it for eternal life. Whoever serves me must follow me; and where I am, my servant also will be. My Father will honor the one who serves me."

JOHN 12:25–26

Each one should test their own actions. Then they can take pride in themselves alone, without comparing themselves to someone else, for each one should carry their own load. Nevertheless, the one who receives instruction in the word should share all good things with their instructor. . . . Let us not become weary in doing good, for at the proper time we will reap a harvest if we do not give up.

GALATIANS 6:4–6, 9

But if serving the LORD seems undesirable to you, then choose for yourselves this day whom you will serve, whether the gods your ancestors served beyond the Euphrates, or the gods of the Amorites, in whose land you are living. But as for me and my household, we will serve the LORD.

JOSHUA 24:15

"Not so with you. Instead, whoever wants to become great among you must be your servant, and whoever wants to be first must be your slave—just as the Son of Man did not come to be served, but to serve, and to give his life as a ransom for many."

MATTHEW 20:26–28

You, my brothers and sisters, were called to be free. But do not use your freedom to indulge the flesh; rather, serve one another humbly in love. For the entire law is fulfilled in keeping this one command: "Love your neighbor as yourself." If you bite and devour each other, watch out or you will be destroyed by each other.

GALATIANS 5:13–15

Worship the LORD with gladness;
    come before him with joyful songs.
Know that the LORD is God.
    It is he who made us, and we are his;
    we are his people, the sheep of his pasture.

PSALM 100:2–3

It is the Lord Christ you are serving. Anyone who does wrong will be repaid for their wrongs, and there is no favoritism.

COLOSSIANS 3:24–25

Serve the LORD with fear
    and celebrate his rule with trembling.

PSALM 2:11

Showing Him to Others

But someone will say, "You have faith; I have deeds."

Show me your faith without deeds, and I will show you my faith by my deeds. . . .

You see that [Abraham's] faith and his actions were working together, and his faith was made complete by what he did. And the scripture was fulfilled that says, "Abraham believed God, and it was credited to him as righteousness," and he was called God's friend. You see that a person is considered righteous by what they do and not by faith alone.

JAMES 2:18, 22–24

For it is by grace you have been saved, through faith—and this is not from yourselves, it is the gift of God—not by works, so that no one can boast. For we are God's handiwork, created in Christ Jesus to do good works, which God prepared in advance for us to do.

EPHESIANS 2:8–10

My dear brothers and sisters, take note of this: Everyone should be quick to listen, slow to speak and slow to become angry, because human anger does not produce the righteousness that God desires. Therefore, get rid of all moral filth and the evil that is so prevalent and humbly accept the word planted in you, which can save you.

Do not merely listen to the word, and so deceive yourselves. Do what it says.

JAMES 1:19–22

Therefore, since we have been justified through faith, we have peace with God through our Lord Jesus Christ, through whom we have gained access by faith into this grace in which we now stand. And we boast in the hope of the glory of God. Not only so, but we also glory in our sufferings, because we know that suffering produces perseverance; perseverance, character; and character, hope.

ROMANS 5:1–4

Finally, be strong in the Lord and in his mighty power. Put on the full armor of God, so that you can take your stand against the devil's schemes. For our struggle is not against flesh and blood, but against the rulers, against the authorities, against the powers of this dark world and against the spiritual forces of evil in the heavenly realms.

Ephesians 6:10–12

That which was from the beginning, which we have heard, which we have seen with our eyes, which we have looked at and our hands have touched—this we proclaim concerning the Word of life. The life appeared; we have seen it and testify to it, and we proclaim to you the eternal life, which was with the Father and has appeared to us. We proclaim to you what we have seen and heard, so that you also may have fellowship with us. And our fellowship is with the Father and with his Son, Jesus Christ.

1 John 1:1–3

We know that we have come to know him if we keep his commands. Whoever says, "I know him," but does not do what he commands is a liar, and the truth is not in that person. But if anyone obeys his word, love for God is truly made complete in them. This is how we know we are in him: Whoever claims to live in him must live as Jesus did.

1 JOHN 2:3–6

Therefore, since we are surrounded by such a great cloud of witnesses, let us throw off everything that hinders and the sin that so easily entangles. And let us run with perseverance the race marked out for us, fixing our eyes on Jesus, the pioneer and perfecter of faith. For the joy set before him he endured the cross, scorning its shame, and sat down at the right hand of the throne of God. Consider him who endured such opposition from sinners, so that you will not grow weary and lose heart.

HEBREWS 12:1–3

God
Walks *with*
Women . . .

Through Heartache

The righteous cry out, and the LORD hears them;
    he delivers them from all their troubles.
The LORD is close to the brokenhearted
    and saves those who are crushed in spirit.
The righteous person may have many troubles,
    but the LORD delivers him from them all.

PSALM 34:17–19

In their hearts humans plan their course,
    but the LORD establishes their steps. . . .
The lot is cast into the lap,
    but its every decision is from the LORD.

PROVERBS 16:9, 33

"Come to me, all you who are weary and burdened, and
I will give you rest. Take my yoke upon you and learn
from me, for I am gentle and humble in heart, and you
will find rest for your souls."

MATTHEW 11:28–29

The LORD is a refuge for the oppressed,
    a stronghold in times of trouble.
Those who know your name trust in you,
    for you, LORD, have never forsaken those who
        seek you.

PSALM 9:9–10

When I called, you answered me;
    you greatly emboldened me. . . .
Though the LORD is exalted, he looks kindly on the
        lowly;
    though lofty, he sees them from afar.
Though I walk in the midst of trouble,
    you preserve my life.
    You stretch out your hand against the anger of my
        foes;
    with your right hand you save me.

PSALM 138:3, 6–7

"The LORD will guide you always;
     he will satisfy your needs in a sun-scorched land
     and will strengthen your frame.
     You will be like a well-watered garden,
     like a spring whose waters never fail. . . .
If you keep your feet from breaking the Sabbath
     and from doing as you please on my holy day,
     if you call the Sabbath a delight
     and the LORD's holy day honorable,
     and if you honor it by not going your own way
     and not doing as you please or speaking idle words,
then you will find your joy in the LORD,
     and I will cause you to ride in triumph on the
          heights of the land
     and to feast on the inheritance of your father
          Jacob."
     For the mouth of the LORD has spoken.

ISAIAH 58:11, 13–14

He heals the brokenhearted
    and binds up their wounds.
He determines the number of the stars
    and calls them each by name.
Great is our Lord and mighty in power;
    his understanding has no limit.
The LORD sustains the humble
    but casts the wicked to the ground.

PSALM 147:3–6

The Spirit of the Sovereign LORD is on me,
    because the LORD has anointed me
    to proclaim good news to the poor.
    He has sent me to bind up the brokenhearted,
    to proclaim freedom for the captives
    and release from darkness for the prisoners.

ISAIAH 61:1

Through Adversity

Dear friends, do not be surprised at the fiery ordeal that has come on you to test you, as though something strange were happening to you. But rejoice inasmuch as you participate in the sufferings of Christ, so that you may be overjoyed when his glory is revealed.

1 PETER 4:12–13

Though I walk in the midst of trouble,
 you preserve my life.
 You stretch out your hand against the anger of my
  foes;
 with your right hand you save me.
The LORD will vindicate me;
 your love, LORD, endures forever—
 do not abandon the works of your hands.

PSALM 138:7–8

Fear of man will prove to be a snare,
  but whoever trusts in the LORD is kept safe.

PROVERBS 29:25

Give us aid against the enemy,
  for human help is worthless.
With God we will gain the victory,
  and he will trample down our enemies.

PSALM 60:11–12

My heart, O God, is steadfast,
  my heart is steadfast;
  I will sing and make music.
Awake, my soul!
  Awake, harp and lyre!
  I will awaken the dawn.
I will praise you, Lord, among the nations;
  I will sing of you among the peoples.

PSALM 57:7–9

Three times I pleaded with the Lord to take [my thorn in the flesh] away from me. But he said to me, "My grace is sufficient for you, for my power is made perfect in weakness." Therefore I will boast all the more gladly about my weaknesses, so that Christ's power may rest on me. That is why, for Christ's sake, I delight in weaknesses, in insults, in hardships, in persecutions, in difficulties. For when I am weak, then I am strong.

2 CORINTHIANS 12:8–10

But thanks be to God, who always leads us as captives in Christ's triumphal procession and uses us to spread the aroma of the knowledge of him everywhere. For we are to God the pleasing aroma of Christ among those who are being saved and those who are perishing.

2 CORINTHIANS 2:14–15

May the LORD bless you from Zion;
        may you see the prosperity of Jerusalem
        all the days of your life.
May you live to see your children's children—
        peace be on Israel.

PSALM 128:5–6

Through Danger

Yes, my soul, find rest in God;
    my hope comes from him.
Truly he is my rock and my salvation;
    he is my fortress, I will not be shaken.
My salvation and my honor depend on God;
    he is my mighty rock, my refuge.
Trust in him at all times, you people;
    pour out your hearts to him,
    for God is our refuge.

PSALM 62:5–8

I call on you, my God, for you will answer me;
    turn your ear to me and hear my prayer.
Show me the wonders of your great love,
    you who save by your right hand
    those who take refuge in you from their foes.
Keep me as the apple of your eye;
    hide me in the shadow of your wings.

PSALM 17:6–8

"When you pass through the waters,
    I will be with you;
    and when you pass through the rivers,
    they will not sweep over you.
    When you walk through the fire,
    you will not be burned;
    the flames will not set you ablaze.
For I am the LORD your God,
    the Holy One of Israel, your Savior;
    I give Egypt for your ransom,
    Cush and Seba in your stead."

ISAIAH 43:2–3

When I am afraid, I put my trust in you.
In God, whose word I praise—
    in God I trust and am not afraid.
    What can mere mortals do to me? . . .
In God, whose word I praise,
    in the LORD, whose word I praise—
in God I trust and am not afraid.
    What can man do to me?

PSALM 56:3–4, 10–11

The LORD is my shepherd, I lack nothing.
He makes me lie down in green pastures,
    he leads me beside quiet waters,
he refreshes my soul.
    He guides me along the right paths
    for his name's sake.
Even though I walk
    through the darkest valley,
    I will fear no evil,
    for you are with me;
    your rod and your staff,
    they comfort me.

PSALM 23:1–4

Who is like the LORD our God,
    the One who sits enthroned on high,
who stoops down to look
    on the heavens and the earth?
He raises the poor from the dust
    and lifts the needy from the ash heap;
he seats them with princes,
    with the princes of his people.

PSALM 113:5–8

Through Impatience

Consider it pure joy, my brothers and sisters, whenever you face trials of many kinds, because you know that the testing of your faith produces perseverance. Let perseverance finish its work so that you may be mature and complete, not lacking anything. If any of you lacks wisdom, you should ask God, who gives generously to all without finding fault, and it will be given to you.

JAMES 1:2–5

He gives strength to the weary
　　and increases the power of the weak.
Even youths grow tired and weary,
　　and young men stumble and fall;
but those who hope in the LORD
　　will renew their strength.
　　They will soar on wings like eagles;
　　they will run and not grow weary,
　　they will walk and not be faint.

ISAIAH 40:29–31

Be patient, then, brothers and sisters, until the Lord's coming. See how the farmer waits for the land to yield its valuable crop, patiently waiting for the autumn and spring rains. You too, be patient and stand firm, because the Lord's coming is near. Don't grumble against one another, brothers and sisters, or you will be judged. The Judge is standing at the door!

JAMES 5:7–9

But you, LORD, are a shield around me,
    my glory, the One who lifts my head high.
I call out to the LORD,
    and he answers me from his holy mountain.
I lie down and sleep;
    I wake again, because the LORD sustains me.

PSALM 3:3–5

I wait for the LORD, my whole being waits,
    and in his word I put my hope.
I wait for the Lord
    more than watchmen wait for the morning,
    more than watchmen wait for the morning.

PSALM 130:5–6

I remain confident of this:
    I will see the goodness of the LORD
    in the land of the living.
Wait for the LORD;
    be strong and take heart
    and wait for the LORD.

PSALM 27:13–14

When God made his promise to Abraham, since there was no one greater for him to swear by, he swore by himself, saying, "I will surely bless you and give you many descendants." And so after waiting patiently, Abraham received what was promised.

HEBREWS 6:13–15

May the God who gives endurance and encouragement give you the same attitude of mind toward each other that Christ Jesus had, so that with one mind and one voice you may glorify the God and Father of our Lord Jesus Christ.

ROMANS 15:5–6

I know that everything God does will endure forever; nothing can be added to it and nothing taken from it. God does it so that people will fear him.

ECCLESIASTES 3:14

But godliness with contentment is great gain. For we brought nothing into the world, and we can take nothing out of it. But if we have food and clothing, we will be content with that.

1 TIMOTHY 6:6–8

For it is commendable if someone bears up under the pain of unjust suffering because they are conscious of God. But how is it to your credit if you receive a beating for doing wrong and endure it? But if you suffer for doing good and you endure it, this is commendable before God. To this you were called, because Christ suffered for you, leaving you an example, that you should follow in his steps.

1 PETER 2:19–21

Through Failure

Command those who are rich in this present world not to be arrogant nor to put their hope in wealth, which is so uncertain, but to put their hope in God, who richly provides us with everything for our enjoyment. Command them to do good, to be rich in good deeds, and to be generous and willing to share. In this way they will lay up treasure for themselves as a firm foundation for the coming age, so that they may take hold of the life that is truly life.

1 TIMOTHY 6:17–19

"Anyone who loves their life will lose it, while anyone who hates their life in this world will keep it for eternal life. Whoever serves me must follow me; and where I am, my servant also will be. My Father will honor the one who serves me."

JOHN 12:25–26

Listen to advice and accept discipline,
    and at the end you will be counted among the
       wise.
Many are the plans in a person's heart,
    but it is the LORD's purpose that prevails.

PROVERBS 19:20–21

But you are a chosen people, a royal priesthood, a holy nation, God's special possession, that you may declare the praises of him who called you out of darkness into his wonderful light. Once you were not a people, but now you are the people of God; once you had not received mercy, but now you have received mercy.

1 PETER 2:9–10

He does not treat us as our sins deserve
    or repay us according to our iniquities.
For as high as the heavens are above the earth,
    so great is his love for those who fear him;
as far as the east is from the west,
    so far has he removed our transgressions from us.

PSALM 103:10–12

Cast your cares on the LORD
and he will sustain you;
he will never let
the righteous be shaken.

PSALM 55:22

Since, then, you have been raised with Christ, set your hearts on things above, where Christ is, seated at the right hand of God. Set your minds on things above, not on earthly things. For you died, and your life is now hidden with Christ in God.

COLOSSIANS 3:1–3

Love never fails. But where there are prophecies, they will cease; where there are tongues, they will be stilled; where there is knowledge, it will pass away. For we know in part and we prophesy in part.

1 CORINTHIANS 13:8–9

God
Encourages
Each Woman
to . . .

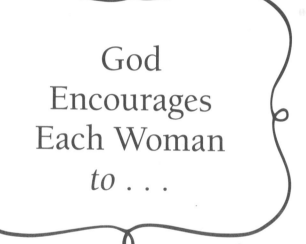

Cherish Being a Friend

Keep on loving one another as brothers and sisters. Do not forget to show hospitality to strangers, for by so doing some people have shown hospitality to angels without knowing it.

HEBREWS 13:1–2

A friend loves at all times,
and a brother is born for a time of adversity.

PROVERBS 17:17

"My command is this: Love each other as I have loved you. Greater love has no one than this: to lay down one's life for one's friends. You are my friends if you do what I command."

JOHN 15:12–14

One who has unreliable friends soon comes to ruin,
    but there is a friend who sticks closer than a
        brother.

PROVERBS 18:24

Do not forsake your friend or a friend of your family,
    and do not go to your relative's house when
        disaster strikes you—
    better a neighbor nearby than a relative far away.

PROVERBS 27:10

Two are better than one,
    because they have a good return for their labor:
If either of them falls down,
    one can help the other up.
    But pity anyone who falls
    and has no one to help them up.
Also, if two lie down together, they will keep warm.
    But how can one keep warm alone?
Though one may be overpowered,
    two can defend themselves.
    A cord of three strands is not quickly broken.

ECCLESIASTES 4:9–12

You, my brothers and sisters, were called to be free. But do not use your freedom to indulge the flesh; rather, serve one another humbly in love. For the entire law is fulfilled in keeping this one command: "Love your neighbor as yourself."

GALATIANS 5:13–14

Be on your guard; stand firm in the faith; be courageous; be strong. Do everything in love.

1 CORINTHIANS 16:13–14

Give to Others with Grace

Let us not become weary in doing good, for at the proper time we will reap a harvest if we do not give up. Therefore, as we have opportunity, let us do good to all people, especially to those who belong to the family of believers.

GALATIANS 6:9–10

"Give, and it will be given to you. A good measure, pressed down, shaken together and running over, will be poured into your lap. For with the measure you use, it will be measured to you."

LUKE 6:38

Those who give to the poor will lack nothing,
    but those who close their eyes to them receive
        many curses.

PROVERBS 28:27

She opens her arms to the poor
    and extends her hands to the needy.
When it snows, she has no fear for her household;
    for all of them are clothed in scarlet.

PROVERBS 31:20–21

This is how we know what love is: Jesus Christ laid down his life for us. And we ought to lay down our lives for our brothers and sisters. If anyone has material possessions and sees a brother or sister in need but has no pity on them, how can the love of God be in that person? Dear children, let us not love with words or speech but with actions and in truth.

1 JOHN 3:16–18

He has shown you, O mortal, what is good.
    And what does the LORD require of you?
    To act justly and to love mercy
    and to walk humbly with your God.

MICAH 6:8

"Anyone who welcomes you welcomes me, and anyone who welcomes me welcomes the one who sent me. Whoever welcomes a prophet as a prophet will receive a prophet's reward, and whoever welcomes a righteous person as a righteous person will receive a righteous person's reward. And if anyone gives even a cup of cold water to one of these little ones who is my disciple, truly I tell you, that person will certainly not lose their reward."

MATTHEW 10:40–42

Finally, all of you, be like-minded, be sympathetic, love one another, be compassionate and humble. Do not repay evil with evil or insult with insult. On the contrary, repay evil with blessing, because to this you were called so that you may inherit a blessing.

1 PETER 3:8–9

Live a Life of Service

"Not so with you. Instead, whoever wants to become great among you must be your servant, and whoever wants to be first must be your slave—just as the Son of Man did not come to be served, but to serve, and to give his life as a ransom for many."

MATTHEW 20:26–28

Whatever you do, work at it with all your heart, as working for the Lord, not for human masters, since you know that you will receive an inheritance from the Lord as a reward. It is the Lord Christ you are serving. Anyone who does wrong will be repaid for their wrongs, and there is no favoritism.

COLOSSIANS 3:23–25

"Whoever can be trusted with very little can also be trusted with much, and whoever is dishonest with very little will also be dishonest with much. So if you have not been trustworthy in handling worldly wealth, who will trust you with true riches? And if you have not been trustworthy with someone else's property, who will give you property of your own?

"No one can serve two masters. Either you will hate the one and love the other, or you will be devoted to the one and despise the other. You cannot serve both God and money."

LUKE 16:10–13

Each of you should use whatever gift you have received to serve others, as faithful stewards of God's grace in its various forms. If anyone speaks, they should do so as one who speaks the very words of God. If anyone serves, they should do so with the strength God provides, so that in all things God may be praised through Jesus Christ. To him be the glory and the power for ever and ever. Amen.

1 PETER 4:10–11

Worship the LORD with gladness;
    come before him with joyful songs.
Know that the LORD is God.
    It is he who made us, and we are his;
    we are his people, the sheep of his pasture.

PSALM 100:2–3

How much more, then, will the blood of Christ, who through the eternal Spirit offered himself unblemished to God, cleanse our consciences from acts that lead to death, so that we may serve the living God!

HEBREWS 9:14

Therefore, I urge you, brothers and sisters, in view of God's mercy, to offer your bodies as a living sacrifice, holy and pleasing to God—this is your true and proper worship. Do not conform to the pattern of this world, but be transformed by the renewing of your mind. Then you will be able to test and approve what God's will is—his good, pleasing and perfect will.

ROMANS 12:1–2

Offer Encouragement

Rejoice with those who rejoice; mourn with those who mourn. Live in harmony with one another. Do not be proud, but be willing to associate with people of low position. Do not be conceited. Do not repay anyone evil for evil. Be careful to do what is right in the eyes of everyone.

ROMANS 12:15–17

For God did not appoint us to suffer wrath but to receive salvation through our Lord Jesus Christ. He died for us so that, whether we are awake or asleep, we may live together with him. Therefore encourage one another and build each other up, just as in fact you are doing.

1 THESSALONIANS 5:9–11

Let us hold unswervingly to the hope we profess, for he who promised is faithful. And let us consider how we may spur one another on toward love and good deeds, not giving up meeting together, as some are in the habit of doing, but encouraging one another—and all the more as you see the Day approaching.

HEBREWS 10:23–25

If we claim to have fellowship with him and yet walk in the darkness, we lie and do not live out the truth. But if we walk in the light, as he is in the light, we have fellowship with one another, and the blood of Jesus, his Son, purifies us from all sin.

1 JOHN 1:6–7

Since, then, you have been raised with Christ, set your hearts on things above, where Christ is, seated at the right hand of God. Set your minds on things above, not on earthly things. For you died, and your life is now hidden with Christ in God. When Christ, who is your life, appears, then you also will appear with him in glory.

COLOSSIANS 3:1–4

Let us therefore make every effort to do what leads to peace and to mutual edification.

ROMANS 14:19

My goal is that they may be encouraged in heart and united in love, so that they may have the full riches of complete understanding, in order that they may know the mystery of God, namely, Christ, in whom are hidden all the treasures of wisdom and knowledge.

COLOSSIANS 2:2–3

Now may the Lord of peace himself give you peace at all times and in every way. The Lord be with all of you.

2 THESSALONIANS 3:16

Pray for One Another

Take the helmet of salvation and the sword of the Spirit, which is the word of God. And pray in the Spirit on all occasions with all kinds of prayers and requests. With this in mind, be alert and always keep on praying for all the Lord's people.

EPHESIANS 6:17–18

Rejoice always, pray continually, give thanks in all circumstances; for this is God's will for you in Christ Jesus.

1 THESSALONIANS 5:16–18

"For the eyes of the Lord are on the righteous
    and his ears are attentive to their prayer,
    but the face of the Lord is against those who
        do evil."
Who is going to harm you if you are eager to do good?

1 PETER 3:12–13

This is the confidence we have in approaching God: that if we ask anything according to his will, he hears us. And if we know that he hears us—whatever we ask—we know that we have what we asked of him.

1 JOHN 5:14–15

In your relationships with one another, have the same mindset as Christ Jesus:
> Who, being in very nature God,
>> did not consider equality with God something
>>> to be used to his own advantage;
> rather, he made himself nothing
>> by taking the very nature of a servant,
>> being made in human likeness. . . .
> Therefore God exalted him to the highest place
>> and gave him the name that is above
>>> every name.

PHILIPPIANS 2:5–7, 9

"Call to me and I will answer you and tell you great and unsearchable things you do not know."

JEREMIAH 33:3

Hear my prayer, LORD;
   listen to my cry for mercy.
When I am in distress, I call to you,
   because you answer me.
Among the gods there is none like you, Lord;
   no deeds can compare with yours.
All the nations you have made
   will come and worship before you, Lord;
   they will bring glory to your name.

PSALM 86:6–9

"I am the LORD, the God of all mankind. Is anything too hard for me?"

JEREMIAH 32:27

Celebrate with Joy

I will give thanks to you, LORD, with all my heart;
  I will tell of all your wonderful deeds.
I will be glad and rejoice in you;
  I will sing the praises of your name, O Most High.

PSALM 9:1–2

In that day they will say,
  "Surely this is our God;
  we trusted in him, and he saved us.
  This is the LORD, we trusted in him;
  let us rejoice and be glad in his salvation."

ISAIAH 25:9

Yet I will rejoice in the LORD,
  I will be joyful in God my Savior.

HABAKKUK 3:18

I will sing of the LORD's great love forever;
>with my mouth I will make your faithfulness
>>known
>through all generations.
I will declare that your love stands firm forever,
>that you have established your faithfulness in
>>heaven itself.
You said, "I have made a covenant with my chosen one,
>I have sworn to David my servant,
'I will establish your line forever
>and make your throne firm through all
>>generations.'"

PSALM 89:1–4

A happy heart makes the face cheerful,
>but heartache crushes the spirit.
The discerning heart seeks knowledge,
>but the mouth of a fool feeds on folly.
All the days of the oppressed are wretched,
>but the cheerful heart has a continual feast.

PROVERBS 15:13–15

Praise be to you, LORD;
> teach me your decrees.

With my lips I recount
> all the laws that come from your mouth.

I rejoice in following your statutes
> as one rejoices in great riches.

I meditate on your precepts
> and consider your ways.

I delight in your decrees;
> I will not neglect your word.

PSALM 119:12–16

Sing the praises of the LORD, you his faithful people;
> praise his holy name.

For his anger lasts only a moment,
> but his favor lasts a lifetime;
> weeping may stay for the night,
> but rejoicing comes in the morning.

PSALM 30:4–5

Send me your light and your faithful care,
    let them lead me;
    let them bring me to your holy mountain,
    to the place where you dwell.
Then I will go to the altar of God,
    to God, my joy and my delight.
    I will praise you with the lyre,
    O God, my God.

Psalm 43:3–4

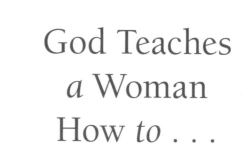

God Teaches *a* Woman How *to* . . .

Trust Him Completely

Trust in the LORD with all your heart
    and lean not on your own understanding;
in all your ways submit to him,
    and he will make your paths straight.

PROVERBS 3:5–6

Trust in the LORD and do good;
    dwell in the land and enjoy safe pasture.
Take delight in the LORD,
    and he will give you the desires of your heart.
Commit your way to the LORD;
    trust in him and he will do this:
He will make your righteous reward shine like the
      dawn,
    your vindication like the noonday sun.

PSALM 37:3–6

Such confidence we have through Christ before God. Not that we are competent in ourselves to claim anything for ourselves, but our competence comes from God. He has made us competent as ministers of a new covenant—not of the letter but of the Spirit; for the letter kills, but the Spirit gives life.

2 Corinthians 3:4–6

My help comes from the Lord,
    the Maker of heaven and earth.
He will not let your foot slip—
    he who watches over you will not slumber;
indeed, he who watches over Israel
    will neither slumber nor sleep.
The Lord watches over you—
    the Lord is your shade at your right hand;
the sun will not harm you by day,
    nor the moon by night.
The Lord will keep you from all harm—
    he will watch over your life;
the Lord will watch over your coming and going
    both now and forevermore.

Psalm 121:2–8

When I saw him, I fell at his feet as though dead. Then he placed his right hand on me and said: "Do not be afraid. I am the First and the Last. I am the Living One; I was dead, and now look, I am alive for ever and ever! And I hold the keys of death and Hades."

REVELATION 1:17–18

In you, LORD, I have taken refuge;
let me never be put to shame.
In your righteousness, rescue me and deliver me;
turn your ear to me and save me.
Be my rock of refuge,
to which I can always go;
give the command to save me,
for you are my rock and my fortress.

PSALM 71:1–3

You will keep in perfect peace
those whose minds are steadfast,
because they trust in you.
Trust in the LORD forever,
for the LORD, the LORD himself, is the Rock eternal.

ISAIAH 26:3–4

GOD TEACHES A WOMAN HOW TO . . .

Hold to Her Faith

Stand firm then, with the belt of truth buckled around
your waist, with the breastplate of righteousness in
place, and with your feet fitted with the readiness that
comes from the gospel of peace. In addition to all this,
take up the shield of faith, with which you can extin-
guish all the flaming arrows of the evil one. Take the
helmet of salvation and the sword of the Spirit, which is
the word of God.

EPHESIANS 6:14–17

But you, dear friends, by building yourselves up in your
most holy faith and praying in the Holy Spirit, keep
yourselves in God's love as you wait for the mercy of our
Lord Jesus Christ to bring you to eternal life.

JUDE vv. 20–21

Consequently, faith comes from hearing the message,
and the message is heard through the word about Christ.

ROMANS 10:17

Therefore we are always confident and know that as long as we are at home in the body we are away from the Lord. For we live by faith, not by sight.

2 CORINTHIANS 5:6–7

For by the grace given me I say to every one of you: Do not think of yourself more highly than you ought, but rather think of yourself with sober judgment, in accordance with the faith God has distributed to each of you. For just as each of us has one body with many members, and these members do not all have the same function, so in Christ we, though many, form one body, and each member belongs to all the others.

ROMANS 12:3–5

But now apart from the law the righteousness of God has been made known, to which the Law and the Prophets testify. This righteousness is given through faith in Jesus Christ to all who believe. There is no difference between Jew and Gentile, for all have sinned and fall short of the glory of God.

ROMANS 3:21–23

Therefore, the promise comes by faith, so that it may be by grace and may be guaranteed to all Abraham's offspring—not only to those who are of the law but also to those who have the faith of Abraham. He is the father of us all.

ROMANS 4:16

May God himself, the God of peace, sanctify you through and through. May your whole spirit, soul and body be kept blameless at the coming of our Lord Jesus Christ. The one who calls you is faithful, and he will do it.

1 THESSALONIANS 5:23–24

GOD TEACHES A WOMAN HOW TO . . .

Have Joy in Him

"Suppose one of you has a hundred sheep and loses one of them. Doesn't he leave the ninety-nine in the open country and go after the lost sheep until he finds it? And when he finds it, he joyfully puts it on his shoulders and goes home. Then he calls his friends and neighbors together and says, 'Rejoice with me; I have found my lost sheep.' I tell you that in the same way there will be more rejoicing in heaven over one sinner who repents than over ninety-nine righteous persons who do not need to repent."

LUKE 15:4–7

"As the Father has loved me, so have I loved you. Now remain in my love. If you keep my commands, you will remain in my love, just as I have kept my Father's commands and remain in his love. I have told you this so that my joy may be in you and that your joy may be complete."

JOHN 15:9–11

Come, let us sing for joy to the LORD;
    let us shout aloud to the Rock of our salvation.
Let us come before him with thanksgiving
    and extol him with music and song.
For the LORD is the great God,
    the great King above all gods.

PSALM 95:1–3

Because your love is better than life,
    my lips will glorify you.
I will praise you as long as I live,
    and in your name I will lift up my hands.
I will be fully satisfied as with the richest of foods;
    with singing lips my mouth will praise you.

PSALM 63:3–5

For the kingdom of God is not a matter of eating and drinking, but of righteousness, peace and joy in the Holy Spirit, because anyone who serves Christ in this way is pleasing to God and receives human approval.

ROMANS 14:17–18

Relent, LORD! How long will it be?

    Have compassion on your servants.

Satisfy us in the morning with your unfailing love,

    that we may sing for joy and be glad all our

        days. . . .

May the favor of the Lord our God rest on us;

    establish the work of our hands for us—

    yes, establish the work of our hands.

PSALM 90:13–14, 17

Open for me the gates of the righteous;

    I will enter and give thanks to the LORD.

This is the gate of the LORD

    through which the righteous may enter.

I will give you thanks, for you answered me;

    you have become my salvation. . . .

The LORD has done this,

    and it is marvelous in our eyes.

The LORD has done it this very day;

    let us rejoice today and be glad.

PSALM 118:19–21, 23–24

Center Her Life in Him

Let the peace of Christ rule in your hearts, since as members of one body you were called to peace. And be thankful. Let the message of Christ dwell among you richly as you teach and admonish one another with all wisdom through psalms, hymns, and songs from the Spirit, singing to God with gratitude in your hearts. And whatever you do, whether in word or deed, do it all in the name of the Lord Jesus, giving thanks to God the Father through him.

COLOSSIANS 3:15–17

I will sing to the LORD all my life;
    I will sing praise to my God as long as I live.
May my meditation be pleasing to him,
    as I rejoice in the LORD.

PSALM 104:33–34

Therefore, there is now no condemnation for those who are in Christ Jesus, because through Christ Jesus the law of the Spirit who gives life has set you free from the law of sin and death. For what the law was powerless to do because it was weakened by the flesh, God did by sending his own Son in the likeness of sinful flesh to be a sin offering. And so he condemned sin in the flesh, in order that the righteous requirement of the law might be fully met in us, who do not live according to the flesh but according to the Spirit.

ROMANS 8:1–4

I sought the LORD, and he answered me;
    he delivered me from all my fears.
Those who look to him are radiant;
    their faces are never covered with shame.
This poor man called, and the LORD heard him;
    he saved him out of all his troubles.
The angel of the LORD encamps around those who
        fear him,
    and he delivers them.

PSALM 34:4–7

For the grace of God has appeared that offers salvation to all people. It teaches us to say "No" to ungodliness and worldly passions, and to live self-controlled, upright and godly lives in this present age, while we wait for the blessed hope—the appearing of the glory of our great God and Savior, Jesus Christ.

TITUS 2:11–13

I pray that out of his glorious riches he may strengthen you with power through his Spirit in your inner being, so that Christ may dwell in your hearts through faith. And I pray that you, being rooted and established in love, may have power, together with all the Lord's holy people, to grasp how wide and long and high and deep is the love of Christ, and to know this love that surpasses knowledge—that you may be filled to the measure of all the fullness of God.

EPHESIANS 3:16–19

I have been crucified with Christ and I no longer live, but Christ lives in me. The life I now live in the body, I live by faith in the Son of God, who loved me and gave himself for me.

GALATIANS 2:20

Now you are the body of Christ, and each one of you is a part of it. And God has placed in the church first of all apostles, second prophets, third teachers, then miracles, then gifts of healing, of helping, of guidance, and of different kinds of tongues. Are all apostles? Are all prophets? Are all teachers? Do all work miracles? Do all have gifts of healing? Do all speak in tongues? Do all interpret? Now eagerly desire the greater gifts.

1 CORINTHIANS 12:27–31

GOD TEACHES A WOMAN HOW TO . . .

Rest in His Protection

The LORD is my light and my salvation—
 whom shall I fear?
 The LORD is the stronghold of my life—
 of whom shall I be afraid?
When the wicked advance against me
 to devour me,
 it is my enemies and my foes
 who will stumble and fall.
Though an army besiege me,
 my heart will not fear;
 though war break out against me,
 even then I will be confident.
One thing I ask from the LORD,
 this only do I seek:
 that I may dwell in the house of the LORD
 all the days of my life,
 to gaze on the beauty of the LORD
 and to seek him in his temple.

PSALM 27:1–4

"Whoever listens to me will live in safety
and be at ease, without fear of harm."

PROVERBS 1:33

The LORD watches over you—
the LORD is your shade at your right hand;
the sun will not harm you by day,
nor the moon by night.
The LORD will keep you from all harm—
he will watch over your life;
the LORD will watch over your coming and going
both now and forevermore.

PSALM 121:5–8

Many, LORD, are asking, "Who will bring us
prosperity?"
Let the light of your face shine on us.
Fill my heart with joy
when their grain and new wine abound.
In peace I will lie down and sleep,
for you alone, LORD,
make me dwell in safety.

PSALM 4:6–8

"No weapon forged against you will prevail,
and you will refute every tongue that accuses you.
This is the heritage of the servants of the LORD,
and this is their vindication from me,"
declares the LORD.

ISAIAH 54:17

"When you pass through the waters,
I will be with you;
and when you pass through the rivers,
they will not sweep over you.
When you walk through the fire,
you will not be burned;
the flames will not set you ablaze.
For I am the LORD your God,
the Holy One of Israel, your Savior;
I give Egypt for your ransom,
Cush and Seba in your stead.
Since you are precious and honored in my sight,
and because I love you,
I will give people in exchange for you,
nations in exchange for your life."

ISAIAH 43:2–4

Obtain His Promises

There the LORD issued a ruling and instruction for them and put them to the test. He said, "If you listen carefully to the LORD your God and do what is right in his eyes, if you pay attention to his commands and keep all his decrees, I will not bring on you any of the diseases I brought on the Egyptians, for I am the LORD, who heals you."

EXODUS 15:25–26

I write these things to you who believe in the name of the Son of God so that you may know that you have eternal life. This is the confidence we have in approaching God: that if we ask anything according to his will, he hears us. And if we know that he hears us—whatever we ask—we know that we have what we asked of him.

1 JOHN 5:13–15

"But seek first his kingdom and his righteousness, and all these things will be given to you as well. Therefore do not worry about tomorrow, for tomorrow will worry about itself. Each day has enough trouble of its own."

MATTHEW 6:33–34

His divine power has given us everything we need for a godly life through our knowledge of him who called us by his own glory and goodness. Through these he has given us his very great and precious promises, so that through them you may participate in the divine nature, having escaped the corruption in the world caused by evil desires.

For this very reason, make every effort to add to your faith goodness; and to goodness, knowledge; and to knowledge, self-control; and to self-control, perseverance; and to perseverance, godliness; and to godliness, mutual affection; and to mutual affection, love. For if you possess these qualities in increasing measure, they will keep you from being ineffective and unproductive in your knowledge of our Lord Jesus Christ.

2 PETER 1:3–8

The LORD your God has increased your numbers so that today you are as numerous as the stars in the sky. May the LORD, the God of your ancestors, increase you a thousand times and bless you as he has promised!

DEUTERONOMY 1:10–11

Against all hope, Abraham in hope believed and so became the father of many nations, just as it had been said to him, "So shall your offspring be." Without weakening in his faith, he faced the fact that his body was as good as dead—since he was about a hundred years old—and that Sarah's womb was also dead. Yet he did not waver through unbelief regarding the promise of God, but was strengthened in his faith and gave glory to God, being fully persuaded that God had power to do what he had promised.

ROMANS 4:18–21

God Blesses
Women When
They . . .

Trust in His Power

Those who trust in the LORD are like Mount Zion,
    which cannot be shaken but endures forever.
As the mountains surround Jerusalem,
    so the LORD surrounds his people
    both now and forevermore. . . .
LORD, do good to those who are good,
    to those who are upright in heart.
But those who turn to crooked ways
    the LORD will banish with the evildoers.
    Peace be on Israel.

PSALM 125:1–2, 4–5

The greedy stir up conflict,
    but those who trust in the LORD will prosper.
Those who trust in themselves are fools,
    but those who walk in wisdom are kept safe.

PROVERB 28:25–26

In the LORD I take refuge.
How then can you say to me:
"Flee like a bird to your mountain.
For look, the wicked bend their bows;
they set their arrows against the strings
to shoot from the shadows
at the upright in heart.
When the foundations are being destroyed,
what can the righteous do?"
The LORD is in his holy temple;
the LORD is on his heavenly throne.
He observes everyone on earth;
his eyes examine them.
The LORD examines the righteous,
but the wicked, those who love violence,
he hates with a passion.
On the wicked he will rain
fiery coals and burning sulfur;
a scorching wind will be their lot.
For the LORD is righteous,
he loves justice;
the upright will see his face.

PSALM 11:1–7

You, LORD, keep my lamp burning;
    my God turns my darkness into light.
With your help I can advance against a troop;
    with my God I can scale a wall.
As for God, his way is perfect:
    The LORD's word is flawless;
    he shields all who take refuge in him.
For who is God besides the LORD?
    And who is the Rock except our God?
It is God who arms me with strength
    and keeps my way secure.

PSALM 18:28–32

My God, I cry out by day, but you do not answer,
    by night, but I find no rest.
Yet you are enthroned as the Holy One;
    you are the one Israel praises.
In you our ancestors put their trust;
    they trusted and you delivered them.
To you they cried out and were saved;
    in you they trusted and were not put to shame.

PSALM 22:2–5

In God, whose word I praise,
in the LORD, whose word I praise—
in God I trust and am not afraid.
What can man do to me?
I am under vows to you, my God;
I will present my thank offerings to you.
For you have delivered me from death
and my feet from stumbling,
that I may walk before God
in the light of life.

PSALM 56:10–13

He will cover you with his feathers,
and under his wings you will find refuge;
his faithfulness will be your shield and rampart.
You will not fear the terror of night,
nor the arrow that flies by day,
nor the pestilence that stalks in the darkness,
nor the plague that destroys at midday.
A thousand may fall at your side,
ten thousand at your right hand,
but it will not come near you.

PSALM 91:4–7

Praise His Goodness

For the LORD takes delight in his people;
>   he crowns the humble with victory.
Let his faithful people rejoice in this honor
>   and sing for joy on their beds.
May the praise of God be in their mouths
>   and a double-edged sword in their hands.

PSALM 149:4–6

My heart, O God, is steadfast,
>   my heart is steadfast;
>   I will sing and make music.
Awake, my soul!
>   Awake, harp and lyre!
>   I will awaken the dawn.
I will praise you, Lord, among the nations;
>   I will sing of you among the peoples.
For great is your love, reaching to the heavens;
>   your faithfulness reaches to the skies.

PSALM 57:7–10

Praise the LORD.

Praise God in his sanctuary;
praise him in his mighty heavens.
Praise him for his acts of power;
praise him for his surpassing greatness.
Praise him with the sounding of the trumpet,
praise him with the harp and lyre. . . .
Let everything that has breath praise the LORD.
Praise the LORD.

PSALM 150:1–3, 6

Because your love is better than life,
my lips will glorify you.
I will praise you as long as I live,
and in your name I will lift up my hands.
I will be fully satisfied as with the richest of foods;
with singing lips my mouth will praise you.

PSALM 63:3–5

"Those who sacrifice thank offerings honor me,
and to the blameless I will show my salvation."

PSALM 50:23

Give thanks to the Lord, for he is good.
His love endures forever.
Give thanks to the God of gods.
His love endures forever.
Give thanks to the Lord of lords:
His love endures forever.
to him who alone does great wonders,
His love endures forever.
who by his understanding made the heavens,
His love endures forever.

Psalm 136:1–5

I will extol the Lord at all times;
his praise will always be on my lips.
I will glory in the Lord;
let the afflicted hear and rejoice.
Glorify the Lord with me;
let us exalt his name together.

Psalm 34:1–3

Hope in His Faithfulness

We are hard pressed on every side, but not crushed; perplexed, but not in despair; persecuted, but not abandoned; struck down, but not destroyed. We always carry around in our body the death of Jesus, so that the life of Jesus may also be revealed in our body. For we who are alive are always being given over to death for Jesus' sake, so that his life may also be revealed in our mortal body.

2 CORINTHIANS 4:8–11

I remain confident of this:
    I will see the goodness of the LORD
    in the land of the living.
Wait for the LORD;
    be strong and take heart
    and wait for the LORD.

PSALM 27:13–14

So do not throw away your confidence; it will be richly rewarded. You need to persevere so that when you have done the will of God, you will receive what he has promised. For,

> "In just a little while,
>> he who is coming will come
>> and will not delay."

And,

> "But my righteous one will live by faith."

HEBREWS 10:35–38

Because of the LORD's great love we are not consumed,
>> for his compassions never fail.

They are new every morning;
>> great is your faithfulness.

I say to myself, "The LORD is my portion;
>> therefore I will wait for him."

The LORD is good to those whose hope is in him,
>> to the one who seeks him;

it is good to wait quietly
>> for the salvation of the LORD.

LAMENTATIONS 3:22–26

For our light and momentary troubles are achieving for us an eternal glory that far outweighs them all. So we fix our eyes not on what is seen, but on what is unseen, since what is seen is temporary, but what is unseen is eternal.

2 CORINTHIANS 4:17–18

For we know that if the earthly tent we live in is destroyed, we have a building from God, an eternal house in heaven, not built by human hands.

2 CORINTHIANS 5:1

Because God wanted to make the unchanging nature of his purpose very clear to the heirs of what was promised, he confirmed it with an oath. God did this so that, by two unchangeable things in which it is impossible for God to lie, we who have fled to take hold of the hope set before us may be greatly encouraged. We have this hope as an anchor for the soul, firm and secure. It enters the inner sanctuary behind the curtain.

HEBREWS 6:17–19

Rest in His Peace

For in the day of trouble
    he will keep me safe in his dwelling;
    he will hide me in the shelter of his sacred tent
    and set me high upon a rock.

PSALM 27:5

Give us aid against the enemy,
    for human help is worthless.
With God we will gain the victory,
    and he will trample down our enemies.

PSALM 60:11–12

The LORD will guide you always;
    he will satisfy your needs in a sun-scorched land
    and will strengthen your frame.
    You will be like a well-watered garden,
    like a spring whose waters never fail.

ISAIAH 58:11

All your children will be taught by the LORD,
  and great will be their peace.
In righteousness you will be established:
  Tyranny will be far from you;
  you will have nothing to fear.
  Terror will be far removed;
  it will not come near you.

ISAIAH 54:13–14

"Come to me, all you who are weary and burdened, and I will give you rest. Take my yoke upon you and learn from me, for I am gentle and humble in heart, and you will find rest for your souls. For my yoke is easy and my burden is light."

MATTHEW 11:28–30

May your unfailing love be my comfort,
  according to your promise to your servant.
Let your compassion come to me that I may live,
  for your law is my delight.

PSALM 119:76–77

The Spirit of the Sovereign LORD is on me,
    because the LORD has anointed me
    to proclaim good news to the poor.
    He has sent me to bind up the brokenhearted,
    to proclaim freedom for the captives
    and release from darkness for the prisoners,
to proclaim the year of the LORD's favor
    and the day of vengeance of our God,
    to comfort all who mourn,
and provide for those who grieve in Zion—
    to bestow on them a crown of beauty
    instead of ashes,
    the oil of joy
    instead of mourning,
    and a garment of praise
    instead of a spirit of despair.
    They will be called oaks of righteousness,
    a planting of the LORD
    for the display of his splendor.

ISAIAH 61:1–3

Stand Strong in the Faith

But you, dear friends, by building yourselves up in your most holy faith and praying in the Holy Spirit, keep yourselves in God's love as you wait for the mercy of our Lord Jesus Christ to bring you to eternal life.

JUDE VV. 20–21

Do not be anxious about anything, but in every situation, by prayer and petition, with thanksgiving, present your requests to God. And the peace of God, which transcends all understanding, will guard your hearts and your minds in Christ Jesus.

PHILIPPIANS 4:6–7

And without faith it is impossible to please God, because anyone who comes to him must believe that he exists and that he rewards those who earnestly seek him.

HEBREWS 11:6

Therefore, since we have been justified through faith, we have peace with God through our Lord Jesus Christ, through whom we have gained access by faith into this grace in which we now stand. And we boast in the hope of the glory of God.

Romans 5:1–2

Yes, my soul, find rest in God;
    my hope comes from him.
Truly he is my rock and my salvation;
    he is my fortress, I will not be shaken.
My salvation and my honor depend on God;
    he is my mighty rock, my refuge.
Trust in him at all times, you people;
    pour out your hearts to him,
      for God is our refuge.

Psalm 62:5–8

"Just as Moses lifted up the snake in the wilderness, so the Son of Man must be lifted up, that everyone who believes may have eternal life in him."

John 3:14–15

But the Lord is faithful, and he will strengthen you and protect you from the evil one. We have confidence in the Lord that you are doing and will continue to do the things we command. May the Lord direct your hearts into God's love and Christ's perseverance.

2 THESSALONIANS 3:3–5

Now faith is confidence in what we hope for and assurance about what we do not see. This is what the ancients were commended for. By faith we understand that the universe was formed at God's command, so that what is seen was not made out of what was visible.

HEBREWS 11:1–3

Claim His Victory

The LORD is close to the brokenhearted
  and saves those who are crushed in spirit.
The righteous person may have many troubles,
  but the LORD delivers him from them all;
he protects all his bones,
  not one of them will be broken.

PSALM 34:18–20

The Spirit himself testifies with our spirit that we are God's children. Now if we are children, then we are heirs—heirs of God and co-heirs with Christ, if indeed we share in his sufferings in order that we may also share in his glory. I consider that our present sufferings are not worth comparing with the glory that will be revealed in us.

ROMANS 8:16–18

He put a new song in my mouth,
>   a hymn of praise to our God.
>   Many will see and fear the LORD
>   and put their trust in him.
Blessed is the one
>   who trusts in the LORD,
>   who does not look to the proud,
>   to those who turn aside to false gods.
Many, LORD my God,
>   are the wonders you have done,
>   the things you planned for us.
>   None can compare with you;
>   were I to speak and tell of your deeds,
>   they would be too many to declare.

PSALM 40:3–5

Great is the LORD, and most worthy of praise,
>   in the city of our God, his holy mountain.

PSALM 48:1

When the perishable has been clothed with the imperishable, and the mortal with immortality, then the saying that is written will come true: "Death has been swallowed up in victory."

"Where, O death, is your victory?
       Where, O death, is your sting?"
The sting of death is sin, and the power of sin is the law.

1 CORINTHIANS 15:54–56

Who may ascend the mountain of the LORD?
       Who may stand in his holy place?
The one who has clean hands and a pure heart,
       who does not trust in an idol
       or swear by a false god.
They will receive blessing from the LORD
       and vindication from God their Savior. . . .
Lift up your heads, you gates;
       be lifted up, you ancient doors,
       that the King of glory may come in.

PSALM 24:3–5, 7

God Comforts
Women
as They
Learn *to* . . .

Handle Spiritual Trials

But he knows the way that I take;
    when he has tested me, I will come forth as gold.
My feet have closely followed his steps;
    I have kept to his way without turning aside.
I have not departed from the commands of his lips;
    I have treasured the words of his mouth more than
        my daily bread.

JOB 23:10–12

Dear friends, do not be surprised at the fiery ordeal that has come on you to test you, as though something strange were happening to you. But rejoice inasmuch as you participate in the sufferings of Christ, so that you may be overjoyed when his glory is revealed. If you are insulted because of the name of Christ, you are blessed, for the Spirit of glory and of God rests on you. . . .

However, if you suffer as a Christian, do not be ashamed, but praise God that you bear that name.

1 PETER 4:12–14, 16

Cast your cares on the LORD
    and he will sustain you;
    he will never let
    the righteous be shaken.

PSALM 55:22

Why, my soul, are you downcast?
    Why so disturbed within me?
    Put your hope in God,
    for I will yet praise him,
    my Savior and my God.

PSALM 43:5

But do not forget this one thing, dear friends: With the Lord a day is like a thousand years, and a thousand years are like a day. The Lord is not slow in keeping his promise, as some understand slowness. Instead he is patient with you, not wanting anyone to perish, but everyone to come to repentance.

2 PETER 3:8–9

Blessed is the one who perseveres under trial because, having stood the test, that person will receive the crown of life that the Lord has promised to those who love him. . . .

Anyone who listens to the word but does not do what it says is like someone who looks at his face in a mirror and, after looking at himself, goes away and immediately forgets what he looks like. But whoever looks intently into the perfect law that gives freedom, and continues in it—not forgetting what they have heard, but doing it—they will be blessed in what they do.

JAMES 1:12, 23–25

I will praise the LORD all my life;
    I will sing praise to my God as long as I live.

PSALM 146:2

But God will redeem me from the realm of the dead;
    he will surely take me to himself.

PSALM 49:15

GOD COMFORTS WOMEN AS THEY LEARN TO . . .

Confront Serious Illness

Have mercy on me, LORD, for I am faint;
>   heal me, LORD, for my bones are in agony.
My soul is in deep anguish.
>   How long, LORD, how long?
Turn, LORD, and deliver me;
>   save me because of your unfailing love.

PSALM 6:2–4

"I have seen their ways, but I will heal them;
>   I will guide them and restore comfort to Israel's
>   mourners,
creating praise on their lips.
>   Peace, peace, to those far and near,"
>   says the LORD. "And I will heal them."

ISAIAH 57:18–19

The Spirit of the Sovereign LORD is on me,
   because the LORD has anointed me
   to proclaim good news to the poor.
   He has sent me to bind up the brokenhearted,
   to proclaim freedom for the captives
   and release from darkness for the prisoners,
to proclaim the year of the LORD's favor
   and the day of vengeance of our God,
   to comfort all who mourn,
and provide for those who grieve in Zion—
   to bestow on them a crown of beauty
   instead of ashes,
   the oil of joy
   instead of mourning,
   and a garment of praise
   instead of a spirit of despair.
   They will be called oaks of righteousness,
   a planting of the LORD
   for the display of his splendor.

ISAIAH 61:1–3

There is a time for everything,
    and a season for every activity under the heavens:
a time to be born and a time to die,
    a time to plant and a time to uproot,
a time to kill and a time to heal,
    a time to tear down and a time to build.

ECCLESIASTES 3:1–3

Praise be to the God and Father of our Lord Jesus Christ, the Father of compassion and the God of all comfort, who comforts us in all our troubles, so that we can comfort those in any trouble with the comfort we ourselves receive from God. For just as we share abundantly in the sufferings of Christ, so also our comfort abounds through Christ.

2 CORINTHIANS 1:3–5

Remember your word to your servant,
    for you have given me hope.
My comfort in my suffering is this:
    Your promise preserves my life.

PSALM 119:49–50

Handle Financial Problems

The Lord answered, "Who then is the faithful and wise manager, whom the master puts in charge of his servants to give them their food allowance at the proper time? It will be good for that servant whom the master finds doing so when he returns. Truly I tell you, he will put him in charge of all his possessions."

LUKE 12:42–44

And my God will meet all your needs according to the riches of his glory in Christ Jesus.

PHILIPPIANS 4:19

Those who trust in their riches will fall,
    but the righteous will thrive like a green leaf.

PROVERBS 11:28

Then Jesus said to his disciples: "Therefore I tell you, do not worry about your life, what you will eat; or about your body, what you will wear. For life is more than food, and the body more than clothes. Consider the ravens: They do not sow or reap, they have no storeroom or barn; yet God feeds them. And how much more valuable you are than birds!"

LUKE 12:22–24

Face the Years Ahead

For none of us lives for ourselves alone, and none of us dies for ourselves alone. If we live, we live for the Lord; and if we die, we die for the Lord. So, whether we live or die, we belong to the Lord.

ROMANS 14:7–8

The righteous will flourish like a palm tree,
　　they will grow like a cedar of Lebanon;
planted in the house of the LORD,
　　they will flourish in the courts of our God.
They will still bear fruit in old age,
　　they will stay fresh and green,
proclaiming, "The LORD is upright;
　　he is my Rock, and there is no wickedness in him."

PSALM 92:12–15

For now we see only a reflection as in a mirror; then we shall see face to face. Now I know in part; then I shall know fully, even as I am fully known. And now these three remain: faith, hope and love. But the greatest of these is love.

1 CORINTHIANS 13:12–13

Our days may come to seventy years,
    or eighty, if our strength endures;
    yet the best of them are but trouble and sorrow,
    for they quickly pass, and we fly away. . . .
Teach us to number our days,
    that we may gain a heart of wisdom. . . .
Satisfy us in the morning with your unfailing love,
    that we may sing for joy and be glad all our
        days. . . .
May your deeds be shown to your servants,
    your splendor to their children.

PSALM 90:10, 12, 14, 16

Teach the older men to be temperate, worthy of respect, self-controlled, and sound in faith, in love and in endurance. Likewise, teach the older women to be reverent in the way they live, not to be slanderers or addicted to much wine, but to teach what is good. Then they can urge the younger women to love their husbands and children.

Titus 2:2–4

But I trust in you, LORD;
    I say, "You are my God."
My times are in your hands;
      deliver me from the hands of my enemies,
      from those who pursue me.

Psalm 31:14–15

I know that my redeemer lives,
    and that in the end he will stand on the earth.
And after my skin has been destroyed,
    yet in my flesh I will see God.

Job 19:25–26

GOD COMFORTS WOMEN AS THEY LEARN TO . . .

Call on God's Divine Protection

In peace I will lie down and sleep,
  for you alone, LORD,
  make me dwell in safety.

PSALM 4:8

Whoever dwells in the shelter of the Most High
  will rest in the shadow of the Almighty.
I will say of the LORD, "He is my refuge and my
      fortress,
  my God, in whom I trust." . . .
He will cover you with his feathers,
  and under his wings you will find refuge;
  his faithfulness will be your shield and rampart.

PSALM 91:1–2, 4

The angel of the LORD encamps around those who
     fear him,
  and he delivers them.

PSALM 34:7

From the west, people will fear the name of the LORD,
     and from the rising of the sun, they will revere his
          glory.
     For he will come like a pent-up flood
     that the breath of the LORD drives along. . . .
"As for me, this is my covenant with them," says the
LORD. "My Spirit, who is on you, will not depart from
you, and my words that I have put in your mouth will
always be on your lips, on the lips of your children and
on the lips of their descendants—from this time on and
forever," says the LORD.

ISAIAH 59:19, 21

Whoever listens to me will live in safety
     and be at ease, without fear of harm.

PROVERBS 1:33

The LORD is my light and my salvation—
    whom shall I fear?
    The LORD is the stronghold of my life—
    of whom shall I be afraid?
When the wicked advance against me
    to devour me,
    it is my enemies and my foes
    who will stumble and fall.
Though an army besiege me,
    my heart will not fear;
    though war break out against me,
    even then I will be confident.
One thing I ask from the LORD,
    this only do I seek:
    that I may dwell in the house of the LORD
    all the days of my life,
    to gaze on the beauty of the LORD
    and to seek him in his temple.
For in the day of trouble
    he will keep me safe in his dwelling;
    he will hide me in the shelter of his sacred tent
    and set me high upon a rock.

PSALM 27:1–5

The LORD watches over you—
the LORD is your shade at your right hand;
the sun will not harm you by day,
nor the moon by night.
The LORD will keep you from all harm—
he will watch over your life;
the LORD will watch over your coming and going
both now and forevermore.

PSALM 121:5–8

Another reason I wrote you was to see if you would stand the test and be obedient in everything. Anyone you forgive, I also forgive. And what I have forgiven—if there was anything to forgive—I have forgiven in the sight of Christ for your sake.

2 CORINTHIANS 2:9–10

God Gives
Freely *to*
Women . . .

Hope for Eternal Life

Sing to the LORD with grateful praise;
     make music to our God on the harp.
He covers the sky with clouds;
     he supplies the earth with rain
     and makes grass grow on the hills.
He provides food for the cattle
     and for the young ravens when they call.
His pleasure is not in the strength of the horse,
     nor his delight in the legs of the warrior;
the LORD delights in those who fear him,
     who put their hope in his unfailing love.
Extol the LORD, Jerusalem;
     praise your God, Zion.
He strengthens the bars of your gates
     and blesses your people within you.

PSALM 147:7–13

Since, then, you have been raised with Christ, set your hearts on things above, where Christ is, seated at the right hand of God. Set your minds on things above, not on earthly things. For you died, and your life is now hidden with Christ in God. When Christ, who is your life, appears, then you also will appear with him in glory.

COLOSSIANS 3:1–4

Know that a person is not justified by the works of the law, but by faith in Jesus Christ. So we, too, have put our faith in Christ Jesus that we may be justified by faith in Christ and not by the works of the law, because by the works of the law no one will be justified. . . .

I have been crucified with Christ and I no longer live, but Christ lives in me. The life I now live in the body, I live by faith in the Son of God, who loved me and gave himself for me.

GALATIANS 2:16, 20

But since we belong to the day, let us be sober, putting on faith and love as a breastplate, and the hope of salvation as a helmet. For God did not appoint us to suffer wrath but to receive salvation through our Lord Jesus Christ. He died for us so that, whether we are awake or asleep, we may live together with him. Therefore encourage one another and build each other up, just as in fact you are doing.

1 THESSALONIANS 5:8–11

But because of his great love for us, God, who is rich in mercy, made us alive with Christ even when we were dead in transgressions—it is by grace you have been saved. And God raised us up with Christ and seated us with him in the heavenly realms in Christ Jesus, in order that in the coming ages he might show the incomparable riches of his grace, expressed in his kindness to us in Christ Jesus.

EPHESIANS 2:4–7

I have fought the good fight, I have finished the race, I have kept the faith. Now there is in store for me the crown of righteousness, which the Lord, the righteous Judge, will award to me on that day—and not only to me, but also to all who have longed for his appearing.

2 TIMOTHY 4:7–8

For those who are led by the Spirit of God are the children of God. The Spirit you received does not make you slaves, so that you live in fear again; rather, the Spirit you received brought about your adoption to sonship. And by him we cry, "*Abba,* Father." The Spirit himself testifies with our spirit that we are God's children. Now if we are children, then we are heirs—heirs of God and co-heirs with Christ, if indeed we share in his sufferings in order that we may also share in his glory.

ROMANS 8:14–17

GOD GIVES FREELY TO WOMEN . . .

Wisdom for Daily Living

My son, pay attention to my wisdom,
    turn your ear to my words of insight,
that you may maintain discretion
    and your lips may preserve knowledge.

PROVERBS 5:1–2

The fear of the LORD is the beginning of wisdom;
    all who follow his precepts have good
        understanding.
    To him belongs eternal praise.

PSALM 111:10

How much better to get wisdom than gold,
    to get insight rather than silver!

PROVERBS 16:16

Blessed are those who find wisdom,
    those who gain understanding,
for she is more profitable than silver
    and yields better returns than gold.
She is more precious than rubies;
    nothing you desire can compare with her.
Long life is in her right hand;
    in her left hand are riches and honor.
Her ways are pleasant ways,
    and all her paths are peace.
She is a tree of life to those who take hold of her;
    those who hold her fast will be blessed.
By wisdom the LORD laid the earth's foundations,
    by understanding he set the heavens in place;
by his knowledge the watery depths were divided,
    and the clouds let drop the dew.
My son, do not let wisdom and understanding out of
       your sight,
    preserve sound judgment and discretion;
they will be life for you,
    an ornament to grace your neck.

PROVERBS 3:13–22

If any of you lacks wisdom, you should ask God, who gives generously to all without finding fault, and it will be given to you. But when you ask, you must believe and not doubt, because the one who doubts is like a wave of the sea, blown and tossed by the wind.

James 1:5–6

"Get wisdom, get understanding;
>   do not forget my words or turn away from them.
Do not forsake wisdom, and she will protect you;
>   love her, and she will watch over you.
The beginning of wisdom is this: Get wisdom.
>   Though it cost all you have, get understanding.
Cherish her, and she will exalt you;
>   embrace her, and she will honor you.
She will give you a garland to grace your head
>   and present you with a glorious crown."
Listen, my son, accept what I say,
>   and the years of your life will be many.
I instruct you in the way of wisdom
>   and lead you along straight paths.

Proverbs 4:5–11

Victory over Sin

Therefore, if anyone is in Christ, the new creation has come: The old has gone, the new is here! All this is from God, who reconciled us to himself through Christ and gave us the ministry of reconciliation: that God was reconciling the world to himself in Christ, not counting people's sins against them. And he has committed to us the message of reconciliation. We are therefore Christ's ambassadors, as though God were making his appeal through us. We implore you on Christ's behalf: Be reconciled to God. God made him who had no sin to be sin for us, so that in him we might become the righteousness of God.

2 CORINTHIANS 5:17–21

It is for freedom that Christ has set us free. Stand firm, then, and do not let yourselves be burdened again by a yoke of slavery.

GALATIANS 5:1

For all who rely on the works of the law are under a curse, as it is written: "Cursed is everyone who does not continue to do everything written in the Book of the Law." Clearly no one who relies on the law is justified before God, because "the righteous will live by faith."

GALATIANS 3:10–11

This is the message we have heard from him and declare to you: God is light; in him there is no darkness at all. If we claim to have fellowship with him and yet walk in the darkness, we lie and do not live out the truth. But if we walk in the light, as he is in the light, we have fellowship with one another, and the blood of Jesus, his Son, purifies us from all sin.

If we claim to be without sin, we deceive ourselves and the truth is not in us. If we confess our sins, he is faithful and just and will forgive us our sins and purify us from all unrighteousness. If we claim we have not sinned, we make him out to be a liar and his word is not in us.

1 JOHN 1:5–10

Create in me a pure heart, O God,
    and renew a steadfast spirit within me.
Do not cast me from your presence
    or take your Holy Spirit from me.
Restore to me the joy of your salvation
    and grant me a willing spirit, to sustain me.

PSALM 51:10–12

But you know that he appeared so that he might take away our sins. And in him is no sin. No one who lives in him keeps on sinning. No one who continues to sin has either seen him or known him.

Dear children, do not let anyone lead you astray. The one who does what is right is righteous, just as he is righteous.

1 JOHN 3:5–7

I instruct you in the way of wisdom
    and lead you along straight paths.
When you walk, your steps will not be hampered;
    when you run, you will not stumble.
Hold on to instruction, do not let it go;
    guard it well, for it is your life.

PROVERBS 4:11–13

Comfort in Troubled Times

The LORD builds up Jerusalem;
    he gathers the exiles of Israel.
He heals the brokenhearted
    and binds up their wounds.
He determines the number of the stars
    and calls them each by name.
Great is our Lord and mighty in power;
    his understanding has no limit.
The LORD sustains the humble
    but casts the wicked to the ground. . . .
He strengthens the bars of your gates
    and blesses your people within you.
He grants peace to your borders
    and satisfies you with the finest of wheat.

PSALM 147:2–6, 13–14

Turn to me and be gracious to me,
    for I am lonely and afflicted.
Relieve the troubles of my heart
    and free me from my anguish.
Look on my affliction and my distress
    and take away all my sins.

PSALM 25:16–18

Cast all your anxiety on him because he cares for you.

Be alert and of sober mind. Your enemy the devil prowls around like a roaring lion looking for someone to devour. Resist him, standing firm in the faith, because you know that the family of believers throughout the world is undergoing the same kind of sufferings.

And the God of all grace, who called you to his eternal glory in Christ, after you have suffered a little while, will himself restore you and make you strong, firm and steadfast. To him be the power for ever and ever. Amen.

1 PETER 5:7–11

A horse is a vain hope for deliverance;
>   despite all its great strength it cannot save.
But the eyes of the LORD are on those who fear him,
>   on those whose hope is in his unfailing love,
to deliver them from death
>   and keep them alive in famine.
We wait in hope for the LORD;
>   he is our help and our shield.
In him our hearts rejoice,
>   for we trust in his holy name.
May your unfailing love be with us, LORD,
>   even as we put our hope in you.

PSALM 33:17–22

I will be glad and rejoice in your love,
>   for you saw my affliction
>   and knew the anguish of my soul.
You have not given me into the hands of the enemy
>   but have set my feet in a spacious place.

PSALM 31:7–8

"Peace I leave with you; my peace I give you. I do not give to you as the world gives. Do not let your hearts be troubled and do not be afraid."

JOHN 14:27

I will extol the LORD at all times;
 his praise will always be on my lips.
I will glory in the LORD;
 let the afflicted hear and rejoice.
Glorify the LORD with me;
 let us exalt his name together.
I sought the LORD, and he answered me;
 he delivered me from all my fears.
Those who look to him are radiant;
 their faces are never covered with shame.
This poor man called, and the LORD heard him;
 he saved him out of all his troubles.
The angel of the LORD encamps around those who
   fear him,
 and he delivers them.
Taste and see that the LORD is good;
 blessed is the one who takes refuge in him.

PSALM 34:1–8

GOD GIVES FREELY TO WOMEN . . .

Power to Defeat Fear

No, in all these things we are more than conquerors
through him who loved us. For I am convinced that
neither death nor life, neither angels nor demons, neither the present nor the future, nor any powers, neither
height nor depth, nor anything else in all creation, will
be able to separate us from the love of God that is in
Christ Jesus our Lord.

ROMANS 8:37–39

Take delight in the LORD,
    and he will give you the desires of your heart.
Commit your way to the LORD;
    trust in him and he will do this:
He will make your righteous reward shine like the
        dawn,
    your vindication like the noonday sun.

PSALM 37:4–6

You, LORD, keep my lamp burning;
     my God turns my darkness into light.
With your help I can advance against a troop;
     with my God I can scale a wall.
As for God, his way is perfect:
     The LORD's word is flawless;
     he shields all who take refuge in him.
For who is God besides the LORD?
     And who is the Rock except our God?
It is God who arms me with strength
     and keeps my way secure.

PSALM 18:28–32

When Jesus spoke again to the people, he said, "I am the light of the world. Whoever follows me will never walk in darkness, but will have the light of life."

JOHN 8:12

Have no fear of sudden disaster
     or of the ruin that overtakes the wicked,
for the LORD will be at your side
     and will keep your foot from being snared.

PROVERBS 3:25–26

The LORD is my light and my salvation—
 whom shall I fear?
 The LORD is the stronghold of my life—
 of whom shall I be afraid?
When the wicked advance against me
 to devour me,
 it is my enemies and my foes
 who will stumble and fall.
Though an army besiege me,
 my heart will not fear;
 though war break out against me,
 even then I will be confident.
One thing I ask from the LORD,
 this only do I seek:
 that I may dwell in the house of the LORD
 all the days of my life,
 to gaze on the beauty of the LORD
 and to seek him in his temple.
For in the day of trouble
 he will keep me safe in his dwelling;
 he will hide me in the shelter of his sacred tent
 and set me high upon a rock.

PSALM 27:1–5

GOD GIVES FREELY TO WOMEN . . .

Courage to Be Women of Integrity

Let the LORD judge the peoples.
    Vindicate me, LORD, according to my righteousness,
    according to my integrity, O Most High.
Bring to an end the violence of the wicked
    and make the righteous secure—
    you, the righteous God
    who probes minds and hearts.

PSALM 7:8–9

The righteous lead blameless lives;
    blessed are their children after them.

PROVERBS 20:7

I will be careful to lead a blameless life—
  when will you come to me?
  I will conduct the affairs of my house
  with a blameless heart.
I will not look with approval
  on anything that is vile.
  I hate what faithless people do;
  I will have no part in it.
The perverse of heart shall be far from me;
  I will have nothing to do with what is evil.
Whoever slanders their neighbor in secret,
  I will put to silence;
  whoever has haughty eyes and a proud heart,
  I will not tolerate.
My eyes will be on the faithful in the land,
  that they may dwell with me;
  the one whose walk is blameless
  will minister to me.
No one who practices deceit
  will dwell in my house;
  no one who speaks falsely
  will stand in my presence.
Every morning I will put to silence

all the wicked in the land;
I will cut off every evildoer
from the city of the LORD.

PSALM 101:2–8

Blessed is the one
    who does not walk in step with the wicked
    or stand in the way that sinners take
    or sit in the company of mockers,
but whose delight is in the law of the LORD,
    and who meditates on his law day and night.
That person is like a tree planted by streams of water,
    which yields its fruit in season
    and whose leaf does not wither—
    whatever they do prospers.
Not so the wicked!
    They are like chaff
    that the wind blows away.
Therefore the wicked will not stand in the judgment,
    nor sinners in the assembly of the righteous.
For the LORD watches over the way of the righteous,
    but the way of the wicked leads to destruction.

PSALM 1:1–6

An honest witness tells the truth,
    but a false witness tells lies.
The words of the reckless pierce like swords,
    but the tongue of the wise brings healing.
Truthful lips endure forever,
    but a lying tongue lasts only a moment.

PROVERBS 12:17–19

Good will come to those who are generous and lend
        freely,
    who conduct their affairs with justice.
Surely the righteous will never be shaken;
    they will be remembered forever.
They will have no fear of bad news;
    their hearts are steadfast, trusting in the LORD.

PSALM 112:5–7

If I have walked with falsehood
    or my foot has hurried after deceit—
let God weigh me in honest scales
    and he will know that I am blameless.

JOB 31:5–6

God Helps
Women *to*
Grow *by* . . .

Recognizing Evil

"Watch out for false prophets. They come to you in sheep's clothing, but inwardly they are ferocious wolves. By their fruit you will recognize them. Do people pick grapes from thornbushes, or figs from thistles? Likewise, every good tree bears good fruit, but a bad tree bears bad fruit. A good tree cannot bear bad fruit, and a bad tree cannot bear good fruit. Every tree that does not bear good fruit is cut down and thrown into the fire. Thus, by their fruit you will recognize them."

MATTHEW 7:15–20

This is how you can recognize the Spirit of God: Every spirit that acknowledges that Jesus Christ has come in the flesh is from God, but every spirit that does not acknowledge Jesus is not from God. This is the spirit of the antichrist, which you have heard is coming and even now is already in the world.

1 JOHN 4:2–3

There is a way that appears to be right,
    but in the end it leads to death.

PROVERBS 14:12

To the pure, all things are pure, but to those who are corrupted and do not believe, nothing is pure. In fact, both their minds and consciences are corrupted. They claim to know God, but by their actions they deny him. They are detestable, disobedient and unfit for doing anything good.

TITUS 1:15–16

Dear friends, although I was very eager to write to you about the salvation we share, I felt compelled to write and urge you to contend for the faith that was once for all entrusted to God's holy people. For certain individuals whose condemnation was written about long ago have secretly slipped in among you. They are ungodly people, who pervert the grace of our God into a license for immorality and deny Jesus Christ our only Sovereign and Lord.

JUDE VV. 3–4

I say this because many deceivers, who do not acknowledge Jesus Christ as coming in the flesh, have gone out into the world. Any such person is the deceiver and the antichrist. . . . Anyone who runs ahead and does not continue in the teaching of Christ does not have God; whoever continues in the teaching has both the Father and the Son. If anyone comes to you and does not bring this teaching, do not take them into your house or welcome them. Anyone who welcomes them shares in their wicked work.

2 JOHN VV. 7, 9–11

For God is not a God of disorder but of peace—as in all the congregations of the Lord's people.

1 CORINTHIANS 14:33

Your word is a lamp for my feet,
    a light on my path. . . .
Your statutes are my heritage forever;
    they are the joy of my heart.
My heart is set on keeping your decrees
    to the very end.

PSALM 119:105, 111–112

Controlling the Tongue

Do not let any unwholesome talk come out of your mouths, but only what is helpful for building others up according to their needs, that it may benefit those who listen. And do not grieve the Holy Spirit of God, with whom you were sealed for the day of redemption. Get rid of all bitterness, rage and anger, brawling and slander, along with every form of malice. Be kind and compassionate to one another, forgiving each other, just as in Christ God forgave you.

EPHESIANS 4:29–32

As long as I have life within me,
    the breath of God in my nostrils,
my lips will not say anything wicked,
    and my tongue will not utter lies.

JOB 27:3–4

Do not repay evil with evil or insult with insult. On the contrary, repay evil with blessing, because to this you were called so that you may inherit a blessing. For,

"Whoever would love life
    and see good days
    must keep their tongue from evil
    and their lips from deceitful speech.
They must turn from evil and do good;
    they must seek peace and pursue it.
For the eyes of the Lord are on the righteous
    and his ears are attentive to their prayer,
    but the face of the Lord is against those
        who do evil."

1 PETER 3:9–12

Do not testify against your neighbor without cause—
    would you use your lips to mislead?
Do not say, "I'll do to them as they have done to me;
    I'll pay them back for what they did."

PROVERBS 24:28–29

One who is wise can go up against the city of the
        mighty
    and pull down the stronghold in which they trust.
Those who guard their mouths and their tongues
    keep themselves from calamity.

PROVERBS 21:22–23

"A good man brings good things out of the good stored
up in his heart, and an evil man brings evil things out
of the evil stored up in his heart. For the mouth speaks
what the heart is full of."

LUKE 6:45

Those who consider themselves religious and yet do not
keep a tight rein on their tongues deceive themselves,
and their religion is worthless.

JAMES 1:26

"Those who sacrifice thank offerings honor me,
    and to the blameless I will show my salvation."

PSALM 50:23

Putting Aside Pride

"Not so with you. Instead, whoever wants to become great among you must be your servant, and whoever wants to be first must be your slave."

MATTHEW 20:26–27

In the same way, you who are younger, submit your-selves to your elders. All of you, clothe yourselves with humility toward one another, because,

> "God opposes the proud
>   but shows favor to the humble."

Humble yourselves, therefore, under God's mighty hand, that he may lift you up in due time.

1 PETER 5:5–6

Pride brings a person low,
    but the lowly in spirit gain honor.

PROVERBS 29:23

Humility is the fear of the LORD;
    its wages are riches and honor and life.

PROVERBS 22:4

Though the LORD is exalted, he looks kindly on the
        lowly;
    though lofty, he sees them from afar.
Though I walk in the midst of trouble,
    you preserve my life.
    You stretch out your hand against the anger of my
        foes;
    with your right hand you save me.

PSALM 138:6–7

Pride goes before destruction,
    a haughty spirit before a fall.
Better to be lowly in spirit along with the oppressed
    than to share plunder with the proud.
Whoever gives heed to instruction prospers,
    and blessed is the one who trusts in the LORD.

PROVERBS 16:18–20

Therefore, as God's chosen people, holy and dearly loved, clothe yourselves with compassion, kindness, humility, gentleness and patience.

COLOSSIANS 3:12

But, "Let the one who boasts boast in the Lord." For it is not the one who commends himself who is approved, but the one whom the Lord commends.

2 CORINTHIANS 10:17–18

As a prisoner for the Lord, then, I urge you to live a life worthy of the calling you have received.

EPHESIANS 4:1

Rejoicing in the Lord

Let the message of Christ dwell among you richly as you teach and admonish one another with all wisdom through psalms, hymns, and songs from the Spirit, singing to God with gratitude in your hearts.

COLOSSIANS 3:16

Nehemiah said, "Go and enjoy choice food and sweet drinks, and send some to those who have nothing prepared. This day is holy to our Lord. Do not grieve, for the joy of the LORD is your strength."

NEHEMIAH 8:10

Restore to me the joy of your salvation
    and grant me a willing spirit, to sustain me.
Then I will teach transgressors your ways,
    so that sinners will turn back to you.

PSALM 51:12–13

The Lord has done great things for us,
    and we are filled with joy. . . .
Those who sow with tears
    will reap with songs of joy.
Those who go out weeping,
    carrying seed to sow,
    will return with songs of joy,
    carrying sheaves with them.

Psalm 126:3, 5–6

"His master replied, 'Well done, good and faithful servant! You have been faithful with a few things; I will put you in charge of many things. Come and share your master's happiness!'"

Matthew 25:21

"I have told you this so that my joy may be in you and that your joy may be complete. My command is this: Love each other as I have loved you."

John 15:11–12

Overcoming Worldliness

Therefore, I urge you, brothers and sisters, in view of God's mercy, to offer your bodies as a living sacrifice, holy and pleasing to God—this is your true and proper worship. Do not conform to the pattern of this world, but be transformed by the renewing of your mind. Then you will be able to test and approve what God's will is—his good, pleasing and perfect will.

ROMANS 12:1–2

Then he said to them all: "Whoever wants to be my disciple must deny themselves and take up their cross daily and follow me. For whoever wants to save their life will lose it, but whoever loses their life for me will save it. What good is it for someone to gain the whole world, and yet lose or forfeit their very self?"

LUKE 9:23–25

Do not love the world or anything in the world. If anyone loves the world, love for the Father is not in them. For everything in the world—the lust of the flesh, the lust of the eyes, and the pride of life—comes not from the Father but from the world. The world and its desires pass away, but whoever does the will of God lives forever.

1 John 2:15–17

Set your minds on things above, not on earthly things. . . . Do not lie to each other, since you have taken off your old self with its practices and have put on the new self, which is being renewed in knowledge in the image of its Creator.

Colossians 3:2, 9–10

It teaches us to say "No" to ungodliness and worldly passions, and to live self-controlled, upright and godly lives in this present age, while we wait for the blessed hope—the appearing of the glory of our great God and Savior, Jesus Christ.

Titus 2:12–13

"I have told you these things, so that in me you may have peace. In this world you will have trouble. But take heart! I have overcome the world."

JOHN 16:33

Rather, we have renounced secret and shameful ways; we do not use deception, nor do we distort the word of God. On the contrary, by setting forth the truth plainly we commend ourselves to everyone's conscience in the sight of God.

2 CORINTHIANS 4:2

See what great love the Father has lavished on us, that we should be called children of God! And that is what we are! The reason the world does not know us is that it did not know him. Dear friends, now we are children of God, and what we will be has not yet been made known. But we know that when Christ appears, we shall be like him, for we shall see him as he is. All who have this hope in him purify themselves, just as he is pure.

1 JOHN 3:1–3

God Rejoices
with Women
When They . . .

Join with Other Believers

"You call me 'Teacher' and 'Lord,' and rightly so, for that is what I am. Now that I, your Lord and Teacher, have washed your feet, you also should wash one another's feet. I have set you an example that you should do as I have done for you. Very truly I tell you, no servant is greater than his master, nor is a messenger greater than the one who sent him. Now that you know these things, you will be blessed if you do them."

JOHN 13:13–17

God is faithful, who has called you into fellowship with his Son, Jesus Christ our Lord.

I appeal to you, brothers and sisters, in the name of our Lord Jesus Christ, that all of you agree with one another in what you say and that there be no divisions among you, but that you be perfectly united in mind and thought.

1 CORINTHIANS 1:9–10

Anyone who claims to be in the light but hates a brother or sister is still in the darkness. Anyone who loves their brother and sister lives in the light, and there is nothing in them to make them stumble. But anyone who hates a brother or sister is in the darkness and walks around in the darkness. They do not know where they are going, because the darkness has blinded them.

1 JOHN 2:9–11

"Teacher," said John, "we saw someone driving out demons in your name and we told him to stop, because he was not one of us."

"Do not stop him," Jesus said. "For no one who does a miracle in my name can in the next moment say anything bad about me, for whoever is not against us is for us. Truly I tell you, anyone who gives you a cup of water in my name because you belong to the Messiah will certainly not lose their reward.

"If anyone causes one of these little ones—those who believe in me—to stumble, it would be better for them if a large millstone were hung around their neck and they were thrown into the sea."

MARK 9:38–42

But you are a chosen people, a royal priesthood, a holy nation, God's special possession, that you may declare the praises of him who called you out of darkness into his wonderful light.

1 PETER 2:9

As it is, there are many parts, but one body.

The eye cannot say to the hand, "I don't need you!" And the head cannot say to the feet, "I don't need you!" On the contrary, those parts of the body that seem to be weaker are indispensable, and the parts that we think are less honorable we treat with special honor. And the parts that are unpresentable are treated with special modesty, while our presentable parts need no special treatment. But God has put the body together, giving greater honor to the parts that lacked it, so that there should be no division in the body, but that its parts should have equal concern for each other. If one part suffers, every part suffers with it; if one part is honored, every part rejoices with it.

Now you are the body of Christ, and each one of you is a part of it.

1 CORINTHIANS 12:20–27

Seek to Understand God's Ways

"Leave your simple ways and you will live;
> walk in the way of insight." . . .
The fear of the LORD is the beginning of wisdom,
> and knowledge of the Holy One is understanding.
For through wisdom your days will be many,
> and years will be added to your life.
If you are wise, your wisdom will reward you;
> if you are a mocker, you alone will suffer.

PROVERBS 9:6, 10–12

How much better to get wisdom than gold,
> to get insight rather than silver!
The highway of the upright avoids evil;
> those who guard their ways preserve their lives.

PROVERBS 16:16–17

Seek the Lord while he may be found;
    call on him while he is near. . . .
"For my thoughts are not your thoughts,
    neither are your ways my ways,"
    declares the Lord.
"As the heavens are higher than the earth,
    so are my ways higher than your ways
    and my thoughts than your thoughts."

Isaiah 55:6, 8–9

If any of you lacks wisdom, you should ask God, who
gives generously to all without finding fault, and it will
be given to you. But when you ask, you must believe and
not doubt, because the one who doubts is like a wave
of the sea, blown and tossed by the wind. That person
should not expect to receive anything from the Lord.

James 1:5–7

For the Lord gives wisdom;
    from his mouth come knowledge and understanding.
He holds success in store for the upright,
    he is a shield to those whose walk is blameless.

Proverbs 2:6–7

Cause

...e to understand the way of your precepts,
    that I may meditate on your wonderful deeds. . . .
Give me understanding, so that I may keep your law
    and obey it with all my heart. . . .
Your hands made me and formed me;
    give me understanding to learn your
        commands. . . .
I gain understanding from your precepts;
    therefore I hate every wrong path.
Your word is a lamp for my feet,
    a light on my path. . . .
I am your servant; give me discernment
    that I may understand your statutes.

PSALM 119:27, 34, 73, 104–105, 125

But it is the spirit in a person,
    the breath of the Almighty, that gives them
        understanding.
It is not only the old who are wise,
    not only the aged who understand what is right.
Therefore I say: Listen to me;
    I too will tell you what I know.

JOB 32:8–10

Stand in Awe of the Lord

And if you look for it [understanding] as for silver
    and search for it as for hidden treasure,
then you will understand the fear of the LORD
    and find the knowledge of God.

PROVERBS 2:4–5

Then those who feared the LORD talked with each other,
and the LORD listened and heard. A scroll of remembrance was written in his presence concerning those
who feared the LORD and honored his name.

"On the day when I act," says the LORD Almighty,
"they will be my treasured possession. I will spare them,
just as a father has compassion and spares his son who
serves him."

MALACHI 3:16–17

The fear of the LORD leads to life;
    then one rests content, untouched by trouble.

PROVERBS 19:23

Now all has been heard;
here is the conclusion of the matter:
Fear God and keep his commandments,
for this is the duty of all mankind.
For God will bring every deed into judgment,
including every hidden thing,
whether it is good or evil.

ECCLESIASTES 12:13–14

Whoever fears the LORD has a secure fortress,
and for their children it will be a refuge.
The fear of the LORD is a fountain of life,
turning a person from the snares of death.

PROVERBS 14:26–27

Praise the LORD.
Blessed are those who fear the LORD,
who find great delight in his commands.
Their children will be mighty in the land;
the generation of the upright will be blessed.
Wealth and riches are in their houses,
and their righteousness endures forever.

PSALM 112:1–3

Seek His Sovereignty

For the LORD is our judge,
>   the LORD is our lawgiver,
>   the LORD is our king;
>   it is he who will save us.

ISAIAH 33:22

Moses said to God, "Suppose I go to the Israelites and say to them, 'The God of your fathers has sent me to you,' and they ask me, 'What is his name?' Then what shall I tell them?"

God said to Moses, "I AM WHO I AM. This is what you are to say to the Israelites: 'I AM has sent me to you.'"

God also said to Moses, "Say to the Israelites, 'The LORD, the God of your fathers—the God of Abraham, the God of Isaac and the God of Jacob—has sent me to you.'

>   "This is my name forever,
>   the name you shall call me
>   from generation to generation."

EXODUS 3:13–15

Great is the LORD and most worthy of praise;
    his greatness no one can fathom.
One generation commends your works to another;
    they tell of your mighty acts. . . .
The LORD is good to all;
    he has compassion on all he has made. . . .
Your kingdom is an everlasting kingdom,
    and your dominion endures through all
        generations.
    The LORD is trustworthy in all he promises
    and faithful in all he does.

PSALM 145:3–4, 9, 13

For this is what the high and exalted One says—
    he who lives forever, whose name is holy:
    "I live in a high and holy place,
    but also with the one who is contrite and lowly
        in spirit,
    to revive the spirit of the lowly
    and to revive the heart of the contrite."

ISAIAH 57:15

The heavens declare the glory of God;
    the skies proclaim the work of his hands. . . .
The law of the LORD is perfect,
    refreshing the soul.
      The statutes of the LORD are trustworthy,
      making wise the simple.
The precepts of the LORD are right,
    giving joy to the heart.
      The commands of the LORD are radiant,
      giving light to the eyes.
The fear of the LORD is pure,
    enduring forever.
      The decrees of the LORD are firm,
      and all of them are righteous.
They are more precious than gold,
    than much pure gold;
    they are sweeter than honey,
    than honey from the honeycomb.

PSALM 19:1, 7–10

"I am the LORD, the God of all mankind. Is anything too hard for me?"

JEREMIAH 32:27

In the beginning God created the heavens and the earth. Now the earth was formless and empty, darkness was over the surface of the deep, and the Spirit of God was hovering over the waters.

And God said, "Let there be light," and there was light.

GENESIS 1:1–3

Oh, the depth of the riches of the wisdom and knowl-
    edge of God!
    How unsearchable his judgments,
    and his paths beyond tracing out!
"Who has known the mind of the Lord?
    Or who has been his counselor?"
"Who has ever given to God,
    that God should repay them?"
For from him and through him and for him are all
    things.
    To him be the glory forever! Amen.

ROMANS 11:33–36

Hope for Revival

"Arise, shine, for your light has come,
   and the glory of the LORD rises upon you.
See, darkness covers the earth
   and thick darkness is over the peoples,
   but the LORD rises upon you
   and his glory appears over you."

ISAIAH 60:1–2

For the earth will be filled with the knowledge of the
      glory of the LORD
   as the waters cover the sea.

HABAKKUK 2:14

"And this gospel of the kingdom will be preached in the
whole world as a testimony to all nations, and then the
end will come."

MATTHEW 24:14

I will declare your name to my people;
in the assembly I will praise you.
You who fear the LORD, praise him!
All you descendants of Jacob, honor him!
Revere him, all you descendants of Israel!
For he has not despised or scorned
the suffering of the afflicted one;
he has not hidden his face from him
but has listened to his cry for help.
From you comes the theme of my praise in the great
assembly;
before those who fear you I will fulfill my vows.
The poor will eat and be satisfied;
those who seek the LORD will praise him—
may your hearts live forever!
All the ends of the earth
will remember and turn to the LORD,
and all the families of the nations
will bow down before him,
for dominion belongs to the LORD
and he rules over the nations.

PSALM 22:22–28

A voice of one calling:

> "In the wilderness prepare
> the way for the LORD;
> make straight in the desert
> a highway for our God.

Every valley shall be raised up,

> every mountain and hill made low;
> the rough ground shall become level,
> the rugged places a plain.

And the glory of the LORD will be revealed,

> and all people will see it together.
> For the mouth of the LORD has spoken."

ISAIAH 40:3–5

The LORD will lay bare his holy arm

> in the sight of all the nations,
> and all the ends of the earth will see
> the salvation of our God. . . .

So he will sprinkle many nations,

> and kings will shut their mouths because of him.
> For what they were not told, they will see,
> and what they have not heard, they will understand.

ISAIAH 52:10, 15

"I will search for the lost and bring back the strays. I will bind up the injured and strengthen the weak, but the sleek and the strong I will destroy. I will shepherd the flock with justice."

EZEKIEL 34:16

"I will show wonders in the heavens
 and on the earth,
 blood and fire and billows of smoke.
The sun will be turned to darkness
 and the moon to blood
 before the coming of the great and dreadful day of
  the LORD.
And everyone who calls
 on the name of the LORD will be saved;
 for on Mount Zion and in Jerusalem
 there will be deliverance,
 as the LORD has said,
 even among the survivors
 whom the LORD calls."

JOEL 2:30–32

Search for Signs of Eternity

But mark this: There will be terrible times in the last days. People will be lovers of themselves, lovers of money, boastful, proud, abusive, disobedient to their parents, ungrateful, unholy, without love, unforgiving, slanderous, without self-control, brutal, not lovers of the good, treacherous, rash, conceited, lovers of pleasure rather than lovers of God—having a form of godliness but denying its power. Have nothing to do with such people.

2 TIMOTHY 3:1–5

Since ancient times no one has heard,
>   no ear has perceived,
>   no eye has seen any God besides you,
>   who acts on behalf of those who wait for him.

ISAIAH 64:4

Jesus answered: "Watch out that no one deceives you. For many will come in my name, claiming, 'I am the Messiah,' and will deceive many. You will hear of wars and rumors of wars, but see to it that you are not alarmed. Such things must happen, but the end is still to come. Nation will rise against nation, and kingdom against kingdom. There will be famines and earthquakes in various places. All these are the beginning of birth pains.

"Then you will be handed over to be persecuted and put to death, and you will be hated by all nations because of me. At that time many will turn away from the faith and will betray and hate each other, and many false prophets will appear and deceive many people. Because of the increase of wickedness, the love of most will grow cold, but the one who stands firm to the end will be saved. And this gospel of the kingdom will be preached in the whole world as a testimony to all nations, and then the end will come."

MATTHEW 24:4–14

"Heaven and earth will pass away, but my words will never pass away."

MATTHEW 24:35

Listen, I tell you a mystery: We will not all sleep, but we will all be changed—in a flash, in the twinkling of an eye, at the last trumpet. For the trumpet will sound, the dead will be raised imperishable, and we will be changed. For the perishable must clothe itself with the imperishable, and the mortal with immortality. When the perishable has been clothed with the imperishable, and the mortal with immortality, then the saying that is written will come true: "Death has been swallowed up in victory."

"Where, O death, is your victory?

Where, O death, is your sting?"

The sting of death is sin, and the power of sin is the law. But thanks be to God! He gives us the victory through our Lord Jesus Christ.

1 CORINTHIANS 15:51–57

Dear friends, now we are children of God, and what we will be has not yet been made known. But we know that when Christ appears, we shall be like him, for we shall see him as he is. All who have this hope in him purify themselves, just as he is pure.

1 JOHN 3:2–3